Claude Monet

Crescent Color Guide to

The IMPRESSIONISTS

Crescent Color Guide to
The IMPRESSIONISTS
Denis Thomas

Crescent Books
New York

To Jackie and Daryoush

All rights reserved. No part of this publication
may be reproduced, stored in a retrieval system,
or transmitted, in any form or by any means,
electronic, mechanical, photocopying, recording
or otherwise, without the permission of The Hamlyn
Publishing Group Limited.

Copyright © The Hamlyn Publishing Group Limited
MCMLXXX

First English edition published by
The Hamlyn Publishing Group Limited
London · New York · Sydney · Toronto
Astronaut House, Feltham, Middlesex, England
Library of Congress Catalog Card Number: 80-65952
ISBN 0-517-31855-5

This edition is published by Crescent Books,
a division of Crown Publishers, Inc.
a b c d e f g h
Phototypeset by Tradespools Limited, Frome, Somerset
Printed by Litografía A. Romero, S. A.
Santa Cruz de Tenerife, Canary Islands (Spain)
D. L. TF. 348 – 1980

Illustrations

Front cover:	Manet. *Argenteuil*, 1874. Musée des Beaux-Arts, Tournai.
Back cover:	Renoir. *Mother and Child*, *c.* 1890. National Gallery of Scotland, Edinburgh.
Endpapers:	Monet. *Le Pont d'Argenteuil*, 1874. Musée du Louvre, Paris.
Title spread:	Degas. *The Dance Foyer at the Opéra*, 1872. Musée du Louvre, Paris (Camondo Collection).
Contents spread:	Renoir. *Children in the Afternoon at Wargemont*, 1884. Nationalgalerie, Berlin.

Contents

What Is
Impressionism?   6

Manet   13

Degas   21

Monet   29

Renoir   37

Pissarro   45

Sisley   53

The Aftermath:
Cézanne, Gauguin
and Van Gogh   59

The Impressionists'
Circle   69

Acknowledgments   80

What is Impressionism?

Boudin. *The Jetty at Deauville*, 1869. It was Boudin who helped to set Monet on his way by introducing him to open-air painting along the Normandy coast. Musée du Louvre, Paris.

To a modern eye, Impressionist paintings are among the most instantly enjoyable of all works of art. No one who enjoys looking at pictures, whether in a scholarly way or as a gallery browser, feels uncomfortable or bewildered in their presence. They represent the pleasurable, undemanding side of life – outings and friendships, walks in the country, river trips, a drink at a bar. The Impressionist manner seems so natural, so 'truthful', that it is hard to think of it as revolutionary, much less as an attitude reaching back to the Renaissance – the idea that painting is, above all else, a matter of seeing. This simple proposition may seem unchallengeable; but the majority of the painters whom we think of as old masters went beyond it, enlarging our understanding of the natural world by introducing elements that the eye does not see: the dimension of insight.

The attraction of Impressionism and its limitations are one and the same. It is a view of the world simply as what we see, not what we think or feel; a surface view, immediate and beguiling, in which solid shapes dissolve in a shower of colours. Monet, its greatest practitioner, sought to paint what he imagined a blind person might see on suddenly regaining his sight. Pissarro urged young painters not to define too closely the outlines of things, since precise drawing 'destroys all sensations'. He added: 'Don't proceed according to rules and principles, but paint what you observe. . . . Paint generously and unhesitatingly, for it is best not to lose the first impression.'

That use of the word 'impression' typifies the manner adopted by Monet, the young Renoir, Sisley and Pissarro himself. It was not yet a vogue term and it tended to have different shades of meaning for different people. At the opposite extreme from Pissarro's use of the term, for example, stands Turner, whose late works, unseen by the public in his lifetime, have been called proto-impressionist, thirty years ahead of his time. Turner would have made no sense of such claims. To him, an 'impression' was what is left in the mind after leaving the scene, a

Caillebotte. *Yachts at Argenteuil*, 1888. It was Caillebotte's collection of his fellow-Impressionists' paintings that formed the basis of the collection of their work in the Louvre. Musée du Louvre, Paris.

powerful recollection rather than a quick, receptive glance.

The word was not new when the critic of *Le Charivari*, Louis Leroy, threw it in the Impressionists' faces. Corot frequently used it to describe his own purposes in landscape. It occurs in Constable's writings; and Monet's friend Jongkind said that with him 'everything lies in the impression'. Its usefulness grew, however, as the cultural ripples from the artistic and social upheavals of the 1870s spread into other fields. Mallarmé came to be known as the Impressionist poet, and Debussy as an Impressionist composer. To the painters, it was a substitute for what are loosely regarded as the classic values which sustained art up to that time. It was essentially a rapid response to things seen, in which the painting, the impression, was the thing, not the subject itself. Hard outlines, precise detail, high finish – these were to be avoided; they had no place in an image so fleetingly yet realistically seen.

The Impressionist eye was both descriptive and non-literal, a conjunction which confused the spectator and irritated the critic. There were no rules or standards to be offered as substitutes for conventional practices. Every painter had a right to make up his own rules, if he needed any. The paint itself, the whole apparatus of making a picture, played a dominant part in the whole. The trick was to give the game away.

How it was done is epitomized, in Monet especially, by an extraordinary care for tone and colour. Light is everywhere, even in shadows; the Impressionist idea of shadow is simply a complementary tone which includes the surrounding primary colours. Much use is made of the white surface of the canvas, rather as in a watercolour, to achieve an all-pervading sense of light. The brushwork tends to consist of small dabs of colour, which work with one another to suggest form.

Manet. *Music in the Tuileries Gardens*, 1862.
The bearded young man in the centre is Manet's
brother Eugène. Behind him, Baudelaire's
features are seen in front of the tree. National
Gallery, London.

Degas. *The Meet, c.* 1867—8.
Degas' interest in horses dates from a stay in
Normandy in 1861. He was one of the first
painters to catch the movement of horses on
canvas. Private Collection.

That the Impressionist method involved an element of hard work is
hinted at in one of Monet's letters, written to his friend Bazille from
Honfleur in 1864. The weather is so beautiful, he tells Bazille, that he is
'going mad', his head spinning because he wants to do everything. He
goes on: 'I want to struggle, destroy and begin again, because one can do
what one wants and understands – I see it all done, completely written
down, when I look at nature. When it comes to getting it down yourself
and you are actually working on it – that's when the going gets rough!'

It helps, when looking at Impressionist pictures, to keep in mind the
acknowledged limitations, while enjoying to the utmost the subtleties and
beauty. Before the nineteenth century was over, the Impressionist
concept was proving inadequate for painters of the quality of Renoir,
Cézanne, Gauguin and Van Gogh. In a manuscript written while he was
in Tahiti, Gauguin put his finger on what he saw as its essence. 'The
Impressionists', he said, 'study colour exclusively for decorative effect,
but without freedom, retaining the shackles of verisimilitude. . . . They
heed only the eye, and neglect the mysterious centres of thought.'

Nevertheless, the movement that was to follow owed much to the
Impressionists. They cleared the path for artists who wanted to go their
own way, rather than work within the conventions of polite, Salon-
dominated taste. Gauguin was speaking for a whole generation when he
asserted that, before his easel 'the painter is not the slave either of the past
or the present, either of nature or his neighbour: he is always himself'.
That would not have been so easily said thirty years earlier, when the
Impressionist revolution began.

Some revolutions are both necessary and inevitable: the Impressionist
revolution was no exception. It was necessary if painting in Europe was to
break away from the postures of institutional classical and Romantic art;
and it was inevitable because, midway through the nineteenth century,
the men and the motivation were at hand. Like other revolutionaries
before them, they were a band of individuals, widely different in character

Manet. *La Servante de Bocks* (The Beer Waitress), 1878–9.
Originally part of a larger canvas, Manet's painting has the spontaneity of a sketch, even to the artful clumsiness of the composition. National Gallery, London.

and background. They were neither of one class nor of one mind. None of them particularly relished a life of poverty and ridicule. A few were protected against starvation by family resources. Others knew hunger, borrowed from friends to keep going, or scratched a living on the edge of the commercial world. Between them they produced work which, in the space of twenty years, helped to change not only the course of Western painting but also the nature of the artist's relationship to his subject, his materials and himself.

The nineteenth century view was practical, solid and complacent, and artists were expected to conform to these characteristics in their work. Their job was seen primarily as recorders who might also be allowed, within seemly limits, to take on the additional role of commentator or moralist. Painters were not expected to agitate, or to challenge the collective view of social and political reality. The Impressionist manner – sketchy, indistinct, apparently undisciplined – was an affront to these values; and when, from time to time, a classical theme made an appearance in an Impressionist work, it seemed provocatively ill-painted, even impertinent. A public accustomed to the graceful academism of Claude or Poussin would find nothing to please them in an Impressionist landscape. Few French gallery-goers would have known of John Constable, even if they felt at home with their own Barbizon painters, who inherited the English master's concept of the 'natural painter'.

The year 1874 stands as the opening of the great Impressionist epoch. In April of that year a group of young French artists who shared, in varying degrees, a feeling of rejection by the art Establishment of the day, held a group exhibition in Paris. Among them were Claude Monet, Auguste Renoir, Camille Pissarro, Paul Cézanne, Edgar Degas and Alfred Sisley. An older painter, Eugène Boudin, joined them out of comradeship. The only woman in the group, Berthe Morisot, braved the risk of antagonizing the Salon, where her work was readily accepted, to exhibit with her friends. With another of their circle, Armand

Degas. *Miss La-la at the Cirque Fernando*, 1879.
Circus performers provided ready subjects for the Impressionists. This example by Degas was exhibited in their fourth exhibition, 1879. National Gallery, London.

9

Guillaumin, they numbered eight out of a total of thirty exhibitors, most of whose names are now forgotten. The exhibition, held in a vacant photographer's studio on the corner of the Boulevard des Capucines, was given a long-winded title suggestive of many hours' fruitless argument: 'Société Anonyme des Artistes Peintres, Sculpteurs, Graveurs, etc.' However, among the paintings on view was one which was destined to give the exhibition a name which would stick. It was by Claude Monet, and it was called *Impression: Sunrise.*

The reception which the exhibition was given seems, in retrospect, hysterical. The gibes of the critics and cartoonists (one of them showed a policeman preventing a pregnant woman from entering the exhibition for fear of injury to her unborn child) fell indiscriminately on the band of painters now dubbed, scoffingly, 'Impressionists'. Amid the uproar, they recognized in that name the description they had been looking for; until then they had regarded themselves primarily as 'realists', taking as their subject-matter the everyday life around them and depicting it on the spot, in deliberately unacademic terms which caught the pace and style of the streets and cafés and the suburban pleasure grounds where they felt at home. Renoir, for one, seized on the new name. It would tell the public exactly what the new painters were up to: 'Here is the kind of painting you won't like. If you come in, so much the worse for you – you won't get your money back!'

In the ensuing hundred years the impact of Impressionist painting on men's minds, and on their minds' eyes, has been such as to leave only the vaguest images to compare it with. In that sudden blaze of light most other painting of the time seems shadowy and dim. The Impressionists were contemptuous of most of it, though they respected their immediate forbears such as Delacroix, Courbet and Corot, all of whom influenced them to some degree and whose names are as lustrous as theirs became. But there is no doubt that the kind of paintings exhibited each year at the Paris Salon, and against which the Impressionists rebelled, were of an almost unrelieved mediocrity. The Salon was both the arbiter and the image of public taste, and the only means by which an aspiring painter could find patrons and win recognition. Since the middle of the seventeenth century it had enjoyed a prestige unrivalled in Europe. Starting as an exhibition reserved exclusively for members of the French Academy, the pet of French royalty and the aristocracy, it had burgeoned into a supposedly democratic institution to which any painter might

Renoir. *Cradle Rock, Guernsey*, 1883. 'It seems more like a landscape by Watteau than something real,' wrote Renoir from Guernsey in September 1883. He was delighted by the bathers, changing and splashing between the rocks. Tate Gallery, London.

Sargent. *Claude
Monet Painting at the
Edge of a Wood, c.*
1887.
This is a memento by
Sargent of his
friendship with Monet,
whom he first met in
1876. Tate Gallery,
London.

submit his work. His chance of being accepted depended on the propriety
of his subject-matter and the seemliness of his technique. He would be
judged by a jury dominated by functionaries and bureaucrats and
presided over by an Academician. Gallery after gallery was hung, two or
three lines deep, with the work of painters who felt no urge to step out of
line. Crowds came to stroll and gossip and compare prices. Ingres, a
revered Establishment painter, called it 'a bazaar in which the tremend-
ous number of objects is overwhelming, and business rules instead of art'.
Charles Baudelaire, a regular reviewer of the Salon between 1845 and
1862, castigated a run-of-the-mill landscape painter, Constant Troyon, as
typifying the 'second-class talents' who were achieving popular success
with a minimum of imagination; 'skill without a soul'.

The exhibitors who commanded the biggest crowds, and prices, in the
Impressionists' lifetime were painters such as Ernest Meissonier, who
specialized in genre and battle scenes executed in finicking detail; Jean-
Leon Gérôme, a sugary Neo-Classicist, and Alexandre Cabanel,
showered with honours in his lifetime and virtually forgotten ever since,
except perhaps as the painter of a voluptuous *Birth of Venus* which
Napoleon III bought from the Salon in 1863, the year of a seminal event
in the development of modern art, the Salon des Refusés.

That spring, the Salon jury rejected over three thousand of the five
thousand paintings submitted. No doubt a majority of these were feeble
or incompetent by any standard, but the sweeping dismissal of so many
artists' works caused an outcry. There was, in effect, nowhere else for an
ambitious artist to exhibit. Painters who held one-man shows at dealers'

galleries were suspect. Manet had just taken the risk of showing a group of his paintings with a dealer called Martinet, which must have prejudiced his chances with the gentlemen of the Salon.

For less daring spirits the Salon was all; rejection amounted to public censure from which there was no redress. The affronted *refusés* sent up a howl of complaint, with the press in support. The hubbub reached the ears of Louis Napoleon, who liked on occasion to simulate a liberality not often evident in his political actions. The Emperor made an unannounced visit to the Salon and declared that most of the rejected paintings might be hung after all, if only so that the public could make up their own minds. He ordered that any of the rejected artists who chose to do so could have their work hung, separately from the Salon, in the adjoining Palais de l'Industrie.

Manet, with three paintings, was among those who took up the challenge. So were Pissarro, also with three, Whistler and Cézanne, with one each. Two of Manet's canvases were exercises in his neo-Velazquez manner. The other was a painting destined to immortalize the Salon des Refusés, as this part of the exhibition was promptly called, and to make Manet's name notorious. The crowds who flocked to see what the fuss was about found themselves confronted by a painting of two young men picnicking in a wooded glade with a pair of female companions, one of whom, stark naked, gazed out of the canvas with an air of mild curiosity.

The artist had called it *Le Bain*, later to be changed to *Le Déjeuner sur l'Herbe*; but soon it was being called other names. 'A practical joke, a shameless sore,' protested one critic. 'An absurd composition,' said another. An English art pundit, P. G. Hamerton, complained that 'some wretched Frenchman' had brutalized a classic theme, adding that 'the nude, when painted by vulgar men, is inevitably indecent'. The Emperor himself agreed, and reportedly struck at Manet's painting with his cane. That gesture seems to bring to a climax the mounting hostility to the new mode. It contains all the attitudes which the young French painters recognized as standing between them and the public: self-righteousness, conservatism, and a feeling of being threatened by the forces of cultural change.

Not all the art world was hostile to the newcomers. One dealer, Arsène Houssaye, wrote that Monet and Renoir were the 'two masters' of the school. Instead of art for art's sake, they talked about nature for nature's sake. He commented on the 'brutal frankness of their brush', and promised that a Renoir *Bather* and *Woman in a Green Dress* by Monet, both in his gallery, would one day hang in the Musée du Luxembourg, when that institution opened its door to the new painters. He was not far wrong. But the reconciliation between the Impressionists and the Establishment was still twenty years away.

Manet

Manet. *Le Déjeuner sur l'Herbe*, 1862–3.
Based on Giorgione's *Fête Champêtre* and on
Raphael's drawing of *The Judgement of Paris*,
Manet's painting caused a furore at the Salon
des Refusés in 1863. Musée du Louvre, Paris.

Manet. *The Absinth Drinker*, 1858–9.
This was the first painting Manet ever submitted
to the Salon (1859). It was rejected. Ny
Carlsberg, Glyptotek, Copenhagen.

To a public brought up to expect a picture to tell a story, or point a moral,
or at the very least to leave the spectator in no doubt what it was about,
the *Déjeuner* was a shock. There were no clues to the artist's intentions.
Perhaps he never had any. The classical references on which Manet had
drawn, notably Giorgione's *Fête Champêtre* in the Louvre, only added to
the critics' exasperation. Their reactions to a work which, a century later,
is recognizably of our own age, shows how deep was the gulf between
what was expected of painters in Manet's time and what he felt to be the
true function of the artist. He knew there was an important fight to be
won, and he saw the real battlefield as the Salon. 'My worst enemies are
forced to look at my pictures there,' he said. On the other hand, he was
genuinely taken aback at the hostile reception to the *Déjeuner*. He did not
see himself as the object of scandal and was distressed to find himself cast
in the role of a publicity-seeking saboteur. He regarded himself as a
serious painter using methods learned or adapted from his studies of the
masters. If his work did not come out like theirs, it was because his
motives were different, not because he was less of an artist.

Manet was far from being a stereotype of the bohemian painter. By
birth and education he belonged to the French upper middle class, and he
made no effort to dress, talk or behave otherwise. He was distinguished by
an ironic detachment which enabled him to stand back from the
involvements which agonized many of his friends, and which from the
beginning gave his work a penetrating realism. At the time of *Le Déjeuner
sur l'Herbe* he was still favourably regarded in polite artistic society. True,
the first picture he ever submitted to the Salon, *The Absinth Drinker* in
1859, had been rejected; but two years later two of his pictures (a portrait
of his parents and *The Spanish Guitarist*) had been accepted. The *Guitarist*
even won him an honourable mention.

In the years that followed, during the gradually accelerating
Impressionist revolution, Manet was frequently accepted at the Salon
– a circumstance which seems to set him apart from Pissarro, Monet,

Cézanne and Sisley, who were carrying on the struggle at a different level. But then, it is the historians who have cast Manet as the leader of the Impressionist movement. He himself had no such pretensions. He belongs with Degas, two years his junior and a kindred spirit in some ways, who used to deny he was an Impressionist at all. And yet Manet's example inspired and encouraged his young contemporaries, especially Monet, Renoir and Sisley, who became known as *la bande à Manet* – Manet's gang. Until Manet suddenly emerged as the most adventurous painter of the age, these young painters had looked to Courbet for their example: Courbet, the archetypal Romantic painter, belligerent, extrovert, a fervent radical, rich in battle honours from skirmishes with the authorities. In the year of the Salon des Refusés, Courbet was forty-four and Manet thirty-one. Of the other Impressionists-to-be, Pissarro was a year older than Manet, Renoir was twenty-two, Monet twenty-three and Sisley twenty-four. After the sensations of the Salon des Refusés, Courbet retreated into middle age and Manet became the automatic leader-figure of the young avant-garde.

Tactfully, or perhaps strategically, Manet submitted for the next year's Salon two paintings of a kind less likely to agitate the jury than the now notorious *Déjeuner*: his *Dead Christ with Angels* and *The Bullfight*. Nevertheless, his treatment of the figure of Christ was attacked hotly for its departures from traditional iconography, and the pair of attendant angels for looking more like winged *midinettes* than celestial beings. Here Manet's realism worked against him, and he committed an almost wilful liberty in depicting the wound in Christ's side on the left instead of the right. Though the characteristically impersonal mood stamps the painting with Manet's intelligence, he soon abandoned religious subjects.

Manet. *Moonlight on the Harbour at Boulogne*, 1869. In 1872 the young dealer Durand-Ruel caught sight of this painting in the studio of Alfred Stevens. He promptly bought it then went to Manet's own studio to buy more. Musée du Louvre, Paris.

Manet. *The Balcony*, 1868–9. Three of Manet's friends, including Berthe Morisot (seated), acted as models for this vaguely mysterious composition. Musée du Louvre, Paris.

Having, in a sense, recovered some credit at the Salon, Manet was ready for his next *coup d'éclat*. On his easel was a finished painting which had he chosen to follow up the *Déjeuner* with a similar gesture in the next year's Salon, might well have been rejected. (He saw the Salon des Refusés as a once-and-for-all sensation, not to be repeated.) Manet held back this new painting for the Salon of 1865, perhaps judging that by then the jury would be starting to reconcile themselves to his more adventurous work. It was a portrait of a young woman lying on a bed, adorned only with a bracelet, earrings, neck ribbon and slipper, her left hand spread over her mons veneris, in an attitude borrowed from Poussin's *Triumph of Flora* in the Louvre. Beyond the bed was a negress bearing a bouquet in a paper wrapping. On the end of the bed a black cat arched its back. Manet called it *Olympia*, perhaps in vague acknowledgment of its classical antecedents, which included Titian and Goya as well as Poussin. A more generally accepted explanation is that it was so named by a friend, the poet Zacharie Astruc, just before being delivered to the Salon. As in the *Déjeuner*, the naked young woman seems deliberately painted to involve the spectator, with a gaze of such worldly unconcern as to be sexually shocking. Manet knew it was his masterpiece.

It was accepted at the Salon. Perhaps Manet's impeccable artistic sources persuaded a majority of the jury to see it, despite its startling modernity, as belonging in the mainstream of European painting. One likes to think that they responded, in spite of their prejudices, to the stunning mastery of the design, in which colours of infinite delicacy are brutally brought up against blacks and near-blacks, the tones abutting against each other with no gradations, the shadows forced back by the light falling on the bed and flesh. Not since the unequivocal nudes of Cranach, 350 years earlier, had a female body been painted with quite such candour. Above all, that self-possessed little face with its incurious gaze has for a hundred years defied men to walk past without returning a glance. Olympia's presence is as spell-binding as one of Baudelaire's women (he was a close friend of Manet) in whom the poet sees 'a fusion of

Manet. *Portrait of Berthe Morisot*, 1872. Manet's relations with Berthe Morisot, herself a gifted artist and exhibitor at the Salon, helped to draw him closer to the Impressionists and their cause. Private Collection.

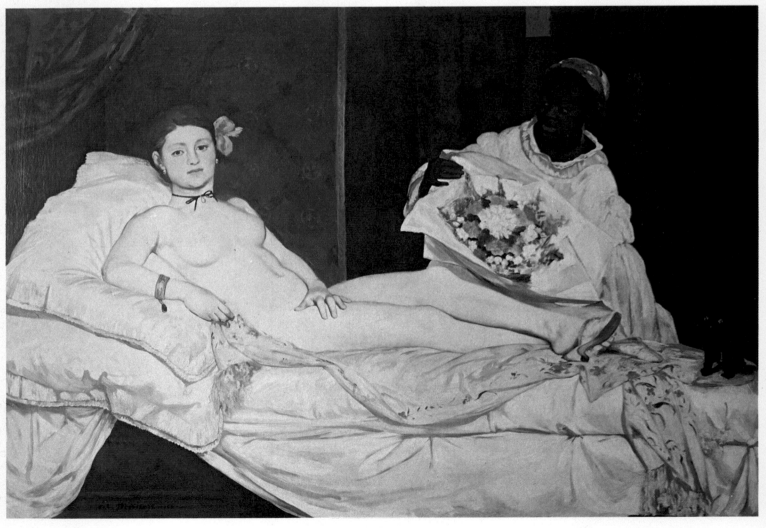

candour and wantonness. . .her arms, her legs, her thighs and her loins glistening as if polished with oil'.

All this, however, meant nothing to the critics. They were horrified by the blatant nudity, the realism, and the assault on the spectator's senses. Some of them recoiled from the painting as if from a dead body, and indeed found corpse-like characteristics in Manet's treatment of the flesh. Théophile Gautier, a distinguished man of letters, wrote: 'Olympia can be understood from no point of view, even if you take it for what it is, a puny model stretched out on a sheet. The colour of the flesh is dirty, the modelling non-existent. The shadows are indicated by more or less large smears of blacking. What is to be said of the negress. . .or for the black cat which leaves its ugly footprints on the bed? We would still forgive the ugliness, were it only truthful. . . . The least beautiful woman has bones, muscles, skin, and some sort of colour.' Courbet remarked, objectively enough: 'It's flat, it isn't modelled; like the Queen of Spades on a playing card just out of her bath.' After the critics came the crowds. Olympia was the only picture they wanted to see. Two guards were posted in front of it to prevent disturbances, and after a couple of days it was moved to a high, inconspicuous position on another wall.

Left:
Manet. Olympia, 1863.
Painted in the same year as the Déjeuner sur l'Herbe, Manet's Olympia achieved a similar sensation at the Salon of 1865. Musée du Louvre, Paris.

Left:
Manet. Chez le Père Lathuile, 1879. One of Manet's perceptive studies of an assignation, painted in 1879. Vibrant brushwork conveys the sexual tension. Musée des Beaux-Arts, Tournai (Collection H. van Cutsem).

With two extraordinary paintings in the space of as many years, Manet had announced the arrival of modern art. What distinguished these works from anything else to be seen in Paris at that time was the sheer painterly quality of Manet's mind and hand. Instead of disguising his arts, as had been the convention among painters for as long as anyone could remember, he blatantly emphasized them. In a painting by Manet the spectator joined in the action. His surfaces were not simulations of real textures: they were unmistakably paint laid on canvas. He was demonstrating that, for the painter, reality consists in attacking his canvas.

It may seem a commonplace a century later; in Manet's time it was a heresy. To disregard perspective, modelling, shading from dark into light – this was an affront to the accepted canons of painting and an insult to all pedagogues. The notion of art as make-believe, or as an experience in which the spectator can allow his mind to penetrate beyond the painter's superficial intention – this too was challenged by Manet's insistence that the viewer should take him literally, compelling him to see the marks he had made on the canvas as well as what those marks stood for. The two great paintings in which he made these intentions plain are revolutionary works of art.

Though Manet's detractors continued to heap insults on his work, a small group of defenders gave him enthusiastic support. Astruc and Baudelaire, and Émile Zola (whose vehement pro-Manet article in the review *L'Evénement* got him the sack) were all active propagandists in his cause. With *la bande à Manet* they became a sort of brotherhood, talking and planning at their favourite meeting place, the Café Guerbois in the Avenue de Clichy. 'Let's go and see Manet,' Pissarro would tell the others, 'he will stand up for us.'

Manet, with his air of slightly dandified distinction, assumed leadership of the group, and embarked on a prolific ten years of painting and drawing which embraced portraits, flower studies, scenes at the races – anything appropriate to his well-known credo: 'Paint what you see – instantly.' When the Union corvette *Kearsarge* engaged the Confederate gun-boat *Alabama* off Cherbourg, he recorded the event with a characteristic sense of drama by going out in a small boat for a closer look. His painting of the action is very different from the conventional heroic composition; it is more like a hurried snapshot, and the more convincing for being viewed from eye-level, with the expanse of sea cramming the subject into the upper third of the picture. In similar response to a news event he painted the execution of the Archduke Maximilian, who after seizing power in Mexico with the help of French troops was promptly left to his fate by Louis Napoleon when the United States protested. Manet, to show his disgust at this betrayal, dressed the firing squad in French uniforms. His debt to Goya's masterpiece, *The Third of May*, is obvious;

but there is a uniquely Manet-like touch in the attitude of the soldier who, standing apart from the death-dealing group, cocks his rifle with professional calm.

By occasionally using another painter's composition as a starting-point for his own, Manet laid himself open to charges of plagiarism. Degas, whose support of Manet was by no means single-minded, said in later years that Manet 'could never do anything but imitate' (though he was also to say 'We never knew how great he was' – a handsome admission from an equal). Manet's use of well-known masterpieces to reinforce his personal response to people, scenes and events can be seen as a means of forcing the viewer to accept the rightness of what he was doing. These painterly quotations have an almost scriptural power, carrying with them the authority of unchallengeable truth.

In what sense, then, can Manet be called an Impressionist painter? In spite of working closely with the Impressionist group and sharing their broad aims, Manet remained very much an individualist. He never abandoned the Salon, and envied the fashionable painters whose work brought them honours and rewards far beyond any which came his way. In a stylistic sense, too, Manet's early work, including the *Déjeuner* and *Olympia*, has nothing in common with what Pissarro, Renoir, Sisley and the rest were doing at the time. He favoured dark backgrounds and sombre blacks, as in the paintings of Velazquez, whom he discovered in the Louvre early in his career. The Impressionists set out by rejecting

Left:
Manet. *Execution of the Emperor Maximilian, c.* 1868. For political reasons, this studiously detached 'protest' painting could not be publicly exhibited at the time (1867–8), though it eventually went on tour in the United States. Städtische Kunstalle, Mannheim. Detail showing a soldier cocking his rifle, *c.* 1867. National Gallery, London.

Left:
Manet. *Nana*, 1877. Nana, the creation of his friend Zola, represented in Manet's version a scandalous glimpse of a courtesan preparing for her client. Kunsthalle, Hamburg.

Manet. *Portrait of the Artist's Parents*, 1860. This unsentimental study of the artist's father and mother was accepted for the Salon of 1861. Private Collection.

black from their palettes altogether; to them shadows were made up of the surrounding tones, never casting sharp lines, softening gradually into lighter shapes.

For all that, they learned from Manet, and Manet learned from them. Though he was a conspicuous absentee from the first Impressionist Exhibition in 1874, in that same year he was painting at Argenteuil on the Seine with Monet, who was living there, and Renoir. Several of Manet's paintings of about this time show an Impressionist influence: a lighter, sunnier palette, stippled brushwork and the distinctive Impressionist sense of airiness. His response to Venice, late in 1874, was markedly Impressionistic and in *Chez le Père Lathuile*, dated 1879, he achieved a fusion of his lifelong attitude to portraiture and the quick, glancing technique of Impressionism as exemplified in similar subjects by Renoir and Monet. By then he had only four years left, in which he moved back to his own personal style in a series of dazzling paintings centred on the Parisian demi-world of bars, circuses, courtesans and night clubs. In 1883, after an operation to amputate a gangrenous leg, in agony and delirium, he died. He was fifty-two.

Degas

Degas. *The Artist's Father Listening to Pagans, c.* 1869–72. The old man's face, as he listens to the guitarist at one of his musical evenings, reflects the painter's sympathetic affection. Musée du Louvre, Paris.

Of Manet's circle the closest to him in age, intellect and temperament was Edgar Degas, whom Manet first met in 1859, the year of his first rejection from the Salon. The two men shared similar social backgrounds: Degas' grandfather had founded a bank and there was plenty of money in the family. He was born in 1834, one of a family of five, to the Creole wife of De Gas *père* (Edgar subsequently spelled his name in the less pretentious form, Degas). His family wanted him to become a lawyer (so had Manet's, offering him the French Navy as a second-best) but he seems to have had little difficulty in getting himself enrolled at the École des Beaux-Arts to study under Louis Lamothe, a former pupil of Ingres. He soon became bored with classwork and repetitive copying in the Louvre, and at the age of twenty-two took himself off to Italy to study the masters.

Degas. *The Bellelli Family, c.* 1860. The Baroness Bellelli was Degas' aunt. Already he was showing an interest in more casual groupings. Musée du Louvre, Paris.

Degas. *Jockeys in the Rain, c.* 1881. Degas was quick to take advantage of the invention of photography. His studies of racehorses have the immediacy of Press photographs. Glasgow Art Gallery and Museum (Burrell Collection).

Back in Paris, he took a studio on the Left Bank and began painting historical subjects. So far he showed no signs of joining the artistic 'underground'; practically the only signs of a response to real events were to be seen in his paintings of the theatre and ballet, a lifelong enthusiasm.

Then came his meeting with Manet. Their talents were of similar kinds, each aiming at directness and simplicity at the expense of finish and detail; the opposite of the conventional picture-making expected of professional painters. Degas sympathized entirely with Manet's impatience with all that was superfluous in a painting. Conciseness, said Manet, was both necessary and elegant: 'The verbose painters are bores.' Degas found Manet's artistic detachment much to his taste, and adopted the same stance in his own work.

Again like Manet, Degas was more at home in the city streets and salons than in the country fields where the Barbizon painters and their heirs found both inspiration and style; and he had an instinctive distaste for the extrovert gestures of Courbet and the Romantic-Realist school which briefly flourished in the glare of his celebrity. He was quite shocked at Manet's respect for official honours. When Manet once recommended him to accept an award, he rounded on him with: 'This isn't the first time I've realized what a bourgeois you are, Manet!' The ambivalent nature of their relationship might also have had something to do with their conflicting political attitudes. Manet, despite his respect for the apparatus of social power, was a convinced republican. Degas was unashamedly a snob. Again, though they shared so much that was important to them as painters, their methods of work were different. Manet believed in putting down what he saw first time. 'If you've got it, that's it.' Degas, on the other hand, said: 'There's nothing less spontaneous than my art.' The brilliant naturalism which he seemed to achieve so easily was the result of deliberation and hard work.

In great artists, human qualities have a way of enlarging themselves through their work, and so it is with Degas. Whatever his public self might have seemed, his private self, the artist, was capable of dignity and compassion surpassing that of moralizing painters such as Millet. In a Degas study of a shopgirl or a laundress or a singer in a café there is an unsentimental tenderness. Like Manet, he did not paint types, he painted

Degas. *Princess Pauline de Metternich, c. 1861–71.* National Gallery, London.

Degas. *Portrait of René Hilaire de Gas*, 1857.
A study of the painter's grandfather. Degas
adopted a less aristocratic version of the family
name. Musée du Louvre, Paris.

real people. In his own life he did not make room for love, or even close
friendship, explaining: 'There is love and there is work, and we have only
one heart.'

His work did not unduly antagonize the jury at the Salon, where he
exhibited regularly after 1865. In 1870 came the war with Prussia,
scattering the band of friends. Degas sailed to the United States, an
experience which excited him (he wrote home about it like any tourist)
and which produced at least one portrait, of Estelle, the blind wife of his
brother Réné, which ranks among his masterpieces. She sits with her
arms folded protectively across her pregnant body, looking into an
endless distance. Another work from this period, *The Cotton Market*, is as
carelessly arranged as a press photograph and with just that kind of
immediacy. It shows his uncle's office in New Orleans, and the figures are
portraits of the family and staff. Degas seemed to revel in the new
possibilities opened up by photography. He delighted in painting from
unconventional angles as if perched on a chair. Ironically, in view of his
obvious attraction to photographic techniques, Degas was suffering from
an eye ailment which partially obscured his vision. One thinks of him
squinting through an imaginary viewfinder, allowing the composition to
assume its involuntary form. He even bought a camera, and used it for
organizing his pictures.

Back in Paris things had changed. The Opéra had been burned down,
depriving Degas of one of his major pleasures and sources of ideas. But

most of the young painters he admired were still there, thinking about
holding a group exhibition. Degas joined them. It was as if, after his
absence, his mind was clear about what he should do next. By joining the
insurgents he was turning his back on a career within the established
professional structure. He ran the same risks as they did, of ridicule and
rejection; and he was not, like most of them, hardened in the fire. He was
not an easy companion, and had little taste for the bohemian hurly-burly
in which they lived. But he gave them his support, and under their
influence his own work became perceptibly higher-keyed, with the bright
colours and shimmering lightness of touch which distinguish Impressionist painting at this, its historical high-water mark.

Degas joined the Impressionists in all but one of their exhibitions; but
meanwhile his own fortunes suffered a severe blow. The family's finances
were found to be in such a tangle after the death of his father that Degas,
to save the family from bankruptcy, sold his own substantial collection of
pictures, only to find that his brother René, husband of Estelle (whom he
afterwards abandoned), was likewise in dire straits following some
unlucky speculations on the stock market. Degas and a brother-in-law
each paid half of what was owing, which effectively reduced Degas to a
financial state not much different from that of his painter friends. Now
dependent on selling his paintings for a living, Degas began to produce
work which, while uncompromisingly his own, compelled the public to
enjoy it.

To these years belong the sketches and paintings of the ballet, in which Degas' enthusiasm and craftsmanship combine so successfully that no major painter has ever again dared to take the ballet as his theme. He grew steadily more successful and respected. As he did so he withdrew from the world. His sight continued to trouble him, and when he found he could no longer manage oils to his satisfaction he turned to a new medium, pastel. Somehow, thanks to a special fixative known only to himself, he transformed pastel into a medium hardly less subtle than watercolour. Instead of his colours turning each other muddy as one was laid over another, Degas was able to achieve miracles of lightness and delicacy which have never been equalled in the medium. He had always been a skilled draughtsman; now, with a crayon in his hand, he became a master. The pleasure these drawings gave, and give still, establishes him among the greatest draughtsmen of modern times. In them he passes beyond the fixed image of the photograph to suggest the next movement, and the one after that, in a single stroke. The dancer's body becomes an instrument, which in her inactive moments she checks and tunes like a violinist.

No one has captured the private moments of a woman, unobserved, absorbed in some female ritual, with such piercing curiosity. To the end Degas retained that essential quality of detachment which he shares with Manet. Other artists, treating such subjects, might become voyeurs. Degas does not react sensually to what he sees and draws; on the contrary, he seems disinterested in the conventional attitudes of coquetry and desire. This gives his figures of women infinitely more interest and,

Degas. *Mlle Malo, c. 1877.*
The Barber Institute of Fine Arts, Birmingham.

Degas. *The Tub*, 1886. Musée du Louvre, Paris.
Degas. *Bed-time*, c. 1883. Tate Gallery, London.
Women's private rituals, as observed by Degas, communicate a unique sense of privacy and drama.

perhaps contrary to his own intentions, an unexpected pathos. It is typical of Degas that he could produce works which give such pleasure without in any way involving himself with the spectator.

'Drawing,' he said, 'is not what one sees but what others have to be made to see.' This is in accord with his belief that art is a sleight of hand by means of which a painter can deceive the spectator into accepting the device as the reality. This brings him nearer to pre-Impressionist attitudes to art than he would perhaps have cared to admit, and certainly it seems a contradiction of Manet's dictum that painting should always look like painting, whatever subject the artist sets himself. But there are many contradictions in Degas, both in his work and his opinions. For instance, he acknowledged the part that a painter's unconscious self plays in helping him create works of art. Only when the artist no longer knows what he is doing, Degas said, does he do good things.

Many of his later works are of this kind; the marvellously gifted practitioner, working at the same familiar subjects over and over again

until they become second nature, can every so often let his unconscious,
poetic self come through. Such moments brought him close to abstract
painting, when as an old man, his sight – like Monet's – grown weak and
unreliable, he painted less what he saw than what he felt to be true.

Degas occupies his own place in the history of European painting,
regardless of his association with the men who called themselves
Impressionists. He refused to be lumped together with them even in the
years when he was closest to them, helping to organize their exhibitions
and showing his own work alongside theirs. He was essentially a non-
joiner, and nearly everything that is known about his private relation-
ships suggests that he was a difficult and sometimes cruel friend. But his
artistic kinship with the Impressionists is real enough. Like them, he took
his subjects from the streets and bars and entertainments of Paris,
without sharing their delight in parks and riverside greenery, farmland
and village landscapes. Like Manet, and like Renoir, he made the human
figure the centre of much of his work and marked his human subjects with
his own signature. He shared with the others an informality of pose and
subject which makes his work easy to receive and enjoy.

While Manet could say, and demonstrate, that a painter's job was to
put down immediately what he saw, Degas insisted that there was
nothing natural about painting. It required, he said, 'as much cunning, as
much malice and as much vice as committing a crime'. He was
nevertheless an Impressionist in a technical sense, an artist more
concerned with the light in which subjects and movements existed than in
the substance. His fascination with light can be seen in the way he used it
to dissolve outlines – as of dancers' dresses – and the distinction he made
between natural brightness and the glare of artificial light. Though he
never painted from nature – his open-air subjects were worked up from
sketches – there is no hint of studio stuffiness in anything he did.

His last years were pitiable. In 1908 his sight failed and he was forced
to give up work altogether. He had never made close friends, nor had he
ever married. Old, nearly blind, rich, revered and alone, he lived on in
Paris, shuffling about the streets with no one to visit and nowhere to go.
At last, on 27 December 1917, he died.

Monet

Monet. *The Gare St-Lazare*, 1877. This painting was the result of a visit by Monet to the Paris railway station, where the station-master obligingly had the engines stoked up to provide maximum atmosphere. Musée du Louvre, Paris.

Claude Monet, Impressionist *par excellence*, owed a lifelong debt to a painter whose work, distinguished as it is, stands outside the Impressionist achievement: Eugène Boudin. When Monet met Boudin at the age of fifteen he was on the brink of becoming a commercial artist. Born in Paris, he had spent his boyhood in Le Havre, where his father was a grocer and ships' chandler. The young Monet exhibited his drawings of local scenes in the window of a local stationer and picture-framer, and it was there that Boudin, who himself found ample subject-matter along the quays and beaches of his native Normandy, noticed Monet's work. He offered advice, and invitations to accompany him on painting excursions. Monet was not much interested to begin with, but suddenly, as he explained in later life, it was 'as if a veil had been removed. The mere example of this artist, devoted to his art and his independent way of life, made me realize what painting could mean.'

More specifically, Boudin showed Monet the subtleties of sunlight and water, and the pleasures of painting out of doors. His parents looked askance at Boudin as a master for their talented son, who was sent instead to Paris to study under one of the leading academic painters of the day, Thomas Couture. Unlike Manet, who spent six years with Couture before finally breaking away, Monet stayed hardly any time at all. He then enrolled at the Académie Suisse, a more free-spirited institution on the Quai des Orfèvres. He met Pissarro there, an association which was to have fruitful consequences for both young men. But before he could make much progress he was called up for military service and shipped off to North Africa.

The experience did him no harm; on the contrary, he declared himself delighted with the light and colour of Algeria. After two years he succumbed to the climate and was sent home. Boudin, who continued to take an interest in him, introduced him to the brilliant young Dutch painter, Jongkind, with whom he found aims and ideas in common. Already Monet was committed to landscape painting. Returning to Paris

Monet. *Jean Monet on his Mechanical Horse*,
1872.
From the Collection of Mr. Nathan Cummings,
New York.

Monet. *The Beach at Trouville*, 1870.
The figures are Monet's bride, Camille, and her
sister, painted just before Monet fled to England
in July 1870. National Gallery, London.

Monet. *Yachts at Argenteuil*, 1875. The pleasures of boating, and the chance to sketch from the open river, were sources of some of Monet's happiest work. Private Collection.

in 1862 he soon made friends with Renoir, Sisley and Bazille, and the four of them practised their shared interest in out-of-doors landscape by painting the forest of Fontainebleau. Monet did not please his parents by associating with these nobodies, and when he refused to enter the prestigious École des Beaux-Arts, as they wished, they cut his allowance. In the 1865 Salon, the year of Manet's notorious *Olympia*, Monet (their names were confused then, as they sometimes are today) showed two seapieces which one critic declared were the best marine paintings in the exhibition. In that year, too, he met a young girl, Camille Doncieux, who became his model and his mistress. In a mounting chaos of poverty and debt, and with Camille pregnant, he burned two hundred of his paintings rather than have them seized by creditors. Then, leaving Camille in Paris, he took refuge with an aunt near Le Havre. From there he bombarded his friends with requests for money, and they responded as best they could.

In April 1869, Boudin visited him and reported to a friend that Monet was 'completely starved, his wings clipped'. The two paintings he had submitted to the Salon had been refused, but he was taking his revenge, Boudin said, by exhibiting at a Paris paint merchants, Letouche, a study of the beach at Sainte-Adresse 'which has horrified his fellow artists'. Boudin added: 'There is a crowd outside the window all the time, and for the young people the generalization of this picture has produced fanatical responses.' Meanwhile Camille had had her baby, Bazille standing as godfather. In June 1870 Monet married her and took her to Trouville, where he painted a carefree beach scene. That same summer the war with Prussia started. Monet fled to England to avoid military service.

He was away for only a year, but his stay in London proved to be one of the formative influences in his career. The mists and melting hues of a northerly landscape were no less suited to Impressionism than the clear, ringing colours of the south. Monet's views of London scenes rank among his most sensitive and successful works – an achievement he shares with Pissarro, who had also fled to London to escape the invasion.

Pissarro joined him in celebrating release from the tensions at home not only by painting but also by seeking out the works of such English masters as Turner and Constable. Later Pissarro was to recall their enthusiasm for London as a painter's subject: 'Monet worked in the parks, while I, living in Lower Norwood, studied the effect of fog, snow and springtime. . . . We also visited the museums. The watercolours and paintings of Constable and Turner and Old Crome certainly had an influence on us. We admired Gainsborough, Lawrence, Reynolds, etc., but we were struck chiefly by the landscape painters who shared more our aim with regard to open-air, light and fugitive effects.' Interesting though

these observations are, Monet and Pissarro are unlikely to have seen the later Turner watercolours, and certainly not the Constable oil sketches, which most powerfully evoke the Impressionist idea to our modern eyes: they were nowhere to be seen in public galleries at that time. It is, however, apparent that these great English painters encouraged them in their exile and reinforced their convictions.

Another unexpected benefit from Monet's spell in London was an introduction, through the French painter Daubigny, to the Paris dealer, Paul Durand-Ruel. He bought pictures from both Monet and Pissarro, paying 200 and 300 francs each for them, five or six times as much as they were used to getting in Paris, and then rarely enough. This is how Monet's friend Armand Silvestre described works like these in 1873, in a note written for the dealer Durand-Ruel: 'Monet loves to juxtapose on the lightly ruffled surface of the water the multi-coloured reflections of the setting sun, of brightly-coloured boats and changing clouds. Metallic tones emitted by the smoothness of the waves, splashing over small, uneven surfaces, are recorded in his work. The image of the shore is vague, the houses broken down as if in a children's game in which objects are assembled from pieces. . . . The pictures are painted in a tonal range, extraordinarily bright. They are pervaded by a blond light – everything is gaiety, clarity, spring festivals and golden evenings. . .windows on to the joyous countryside, on to rivers crowded with pleasure boats, on to a sky that shines with light mists, the life of the outdoors, panoramic and charming.'

British reactions to the work of Monet and Pissarro were more cautious. Neither artist's work was accepted by the Royal Academy during their stay in London. Back in Paris, Monet and the other members of the group found life more difficult than ever. However, they soon reformed, and discussed an idea Bazille had originally suggested for by-passing the Salon and holding their own exhibition. This was the genesis of the Co-operative Society of Artists already described, later to take its name from Monet's *Impression: Sunrise*, painted in 1872.

Certainly it was too much for the Salon to accept, and Monet came to realize the fact. The conflict between his painting and officially recognized standards became impossible to reconcile. He and Renoir, who often painted together in the 1860s, completed the process which had begun a dozen years before, when Edouard Manet drew the crowds to the Salon des Refusés.

For Monet the 1870s were a continual agony. In 1878 a rich new patron, Hoschedé, suddenly went bankrupt. Camille, who had just had a

second child, was unable to recover from the birth. When she died in 1879, Monet set up house with his former patron's widow. It was the turning point in his life. His new wife, a plump and practical thirty-nine-year-old, had a nest-egg of her own. She also had a flair for dressmaking and shrewd management. Monet's pictures began to sell. In 1889 he led a movement to buy Manet's *Olympia* for the Louvre and the following year he bought a solid property at Giverny. The rest of his life brought him continuing esteem as a painter, even if the friends of his youth viewed the later work as a falling-off from painterly values to a kind of exalted decoration.

Monet has been called the most ruthless of the group, the first painter to reject the art of the museums in its entirety. His series of twenty paintings of Rouen Cathedral, in all lights and times of day, is among the most ambitious tasks he ever attempted. He set himself the challenge of making an objective record of fleeting light and atmosphere, as if to prove that there is no contradiction between perceived form and a preconceived manner of seeing. He carried these concepts into his last years, spent in his garden at Giverny with its lake full of lilies and the trailing forms of aquatic vegetation. The Giverny paintings are magically successful in evoking a fusion of elements – domestic, private, yet a universe in themselves.

These water-landscapes, based on sketches done at the pool's edge by a painter whose sight was failing fast, are a combination of outdoor studies and studio work. The outdoor impression was carried indoors, back to the studio; there, after all, the serious work had to be done. Monet has described how, painting these late masterpieces, all of them on a grand scale, his brush went its own way, unguided by anything but the mysterious process of poetic recall. The critic Claude Roger-Marx, reviewing an exhibition of sixty such works in 1909, quoted Monet's 'temptation to decorate a salon with the theme of water lilies, joining them into one – the illusion of a world without end, a sea without horizon or shore'. The realization of this project called for preparations on an heroic scale. He built a huge studio, erected large canvases on specially-constructed easels by the lily ponds, which his gardeners shifted for him as the light changed. A group of nineteen lily-pond paintings was offered

to the French nation in 1917, and a site was found for them in the Orangerie. The National Gallery in London also owns a group, even more loosely painted and seemingly formless, which were found in Monet's studio, apparently forgotten, after his death. It is only in recent times that these works have been comprehensible to visitors: changing taste, and acceptance of abstraction, help towards an understanding of this, the great Impressionist's final statement.

Monet's triumph in the last twenty years of a long life was not lost on some of the rising generation of painters who were destined to carry the new movement into the twentieth century. The young Kandinsky confessed that his eyes had been opened by one of Monet's *Haystacks* when it was exhibited in Moscow in 1895. 'Before, I had known only realistic art. Suddenly, for the first time, I saw a "picture".... What was absolutely clear was the unsuspected power, previously hidden from me, of the palette. Painting took on a fabulous strength and splendour. At the same time, unconsciously, the object was discredited as an indispensable element....' Monet, Cézanne said, was 'only an eye'; adding, 'but what an eye!' It has become his epitaph.

Monet. *The Water-Lily Pond*, 1899. During the last years of his life, with his sight failing, Monet created and immortalized the lily ponds in his garden at Giverny. National Gallery, London.

Renoir

Renoir. *At the Grenouillère*, 1879. *La Grenouillère* (literally, frog-pool), on the Seine at Croissy, was often visited by Renoir and Monet in 1868–9. Here, Renoir uses the sheen of the water to reduce his subject to a surface impression. Musée du Louvre, Paris.

Renoir's position among the Impressionists, like that of Manet and Degas, is somewhat contradictory. On the one hand he produced, over a period of some ten years, works which are the quintessence of Impressionism. On the other hand, he was deeply aware of the long pedigree of European painting, and wanted to be part of it. He revered such masters as Veronese, Titian and (like Manet) Velazquez, and delighted in such eighteenth-century French predecessors as Watteau, Boucher and Fragonard. 'Those bourgeois women of Fragonard's! They are distinguished and at the same time good-natured. You hear them speak the French of our fathers. . . .' When he finished his late masterpiece, *Les Grandes Baigneuses*, he declared: 'Rubens would have been satisfied with it.' For Renoir, there could be no higher satisfaction.

He was born at Limoges, the son of a tailor who brought the family to Paris when Renoir was four. There was no parental resistance to the idea that their son might be a painter. As a first step, he took a job painting flowers on pieces of chinaware for 5 sous a dozen. On evening visits to the Louvre he discovered the masters. Just as he was looking forward to graduating to the rank of porcelain painter at 6 francs a day, a mechanical process was discovered which put his employer out of business. So he took to painting fans, decorating them with copies he made in the Louvre of subjects by Watteau, Lancret and Boucher.

It was not long before he took the logical step of attending art classes. He enrolled with Charles Gleyre, whose pupils included Monet, Bazille and Sisley, and at the École des Beaux-Arts for life drawing and anatomy. His first important paintings were figure subjects and portraits, including a vivid study of Bazille, perhaps the closest friend of his early days. With Monet he often painted on the banks of the Seine. The two men's versions of La Grenouillère in 1869 are strikingly alike with their flickering brushwork, informal composition and sunny colour. Renoir's interest in the human figure seems to have influenced Monet's versions, which in turn made an evident mark on his companion's poetic imagination. Renoir was always impatient of theory, and tended to drop out of earnest conversations which threatened to keep him up late. Composition, he felt, should be as varied as nature. 'The eyes of the most beautiful faces', he observed, 'are always slightly dissimilar. No nose is found exactly above the middle of the mouth. The segments of an orange, the leaves of a tree, or the petals of a flower are never identical.'

Renoir exhibited with his friends at the Impressionist exhibitions of 1874 and 1876, and suffered the general critical mauling. After the second Impressionist exhibition in 1876, the critic of *Le Figaro* penned a scathing notice. 'The innocent passer-by,' he wrote, 'attracted by the flags outside, goes in for a look. But what a cruel sight meets his eyes! Five or six lunatics make up a group of poor wretches who have succumbed to the madness of ambition and dared to put on a show of their work. . . . There is a woman in the group, as in all the best-known gangs. Her name is Berthe Morisot, and she is a curiosity. She manages to convey a certain feminine grace, despite her outbursts of delirium.' The men were furious at these insults to Berthe Morisot, 'that great lady', as Renoir called her. But, as he recalled later, 'she just laughed'.

Though he was as hard-up as Monet, he chose to earn what he could by doing hack work at his old trade. Always the most cheerful and resilient of the group, he revelled in the life of the cafés and boulevards, the river picnics and the company of friends, all of which he celebrated in paint. With Manet and Monet, he brought Impressionism to perhaps its highest pitch of inventive artistry. Monet had a home-made floating studio on the river at Argenteuil. There, Manet painted him at work while Renoir recorded almost identical scenes. Their pictures have more in common than the spirit in which they were painted; the colours are made up of their constituent parts, laid side by side on the canvas, and there are no outlines or hard shadows. Land and water coalesce in a way not seen in

Renoir. *Gabrielle with Roses*, 1911.
By the time he painted this picture, Renoir's work had moved on from pure Impressionism to an almost sculptural sense of solid form. His model, Gabrielle, was the family housemaid at his home in Cagnes. Musée du Louvre, Paris.

Right:
Renoir. *La Loge*, 1874.
Edmond, the painter's younger brother, posed with the model, Nini, in this well-known masterpiece, which was shown at the first Impressionist exhibition of 1874. Courtauld Institute Galleries, London.

Renoir. *Portrait of Monet*, 1875.
Musée du Louvre, Paris.

painting before, yet with brilliant conviction: in Monet's phrase, ensnaring the light and throwing it directly on to the canvas.

Paintings of this character did not find buyers. Renoir's son, Jean, in his biography of his father, tells how all the money the two friends could scrape together went to pay for their studio, a model and coal for the stove. The stove served two purposes: to warm the girls while cooking the food. One of their sitters happened to be a grocer, who paid them in kind. They could make a sack of beans last a month. Renoir said of those days: 'I have never been happier in my life.'

Of his work in those Impressionist years, the *Moulin de la Galette*, exhibited in the 1877 exhibition, is his acknowledged masterpiece. In it, as Renoir's friend Georges Rivière justly observed, there is 'noise, laughter, movement, sun and an atmosphere of youth'. His review went on: 'It is essentially a Parisian work. The girls are the very same who elbow us every day and whose babble fills Paris at certain hours. A smile and a flick of the wrist is enough to be pretty; M. Renoir proves it.' Prophetically, in a reference to the kind of historical subjects which still dominated the Salon, he added: 'When, for the hundredth time, we are shown St. Louis dealing out justice under an oak, are we the better for it? What documents will these artists who deliver us from such lucubrations bequeath to future centuries...?'

The sheer sense of pleasure inherent in Renoir's work might well have been a factor in helping to turn the tide. The Impressionists had no clique to speak up for them. Their friend and champion Émile Zola was for years a lone voice. The praise of other writers came only after they had achieved

Renoir. *At the Piano*, 1892.
The two young girls are Berthe Morisot's daughter Julie and her cousin Paulette. Lehman Collection, New York.

Renoir. *Portrait of Frédéric Bazille*, 1867.
The painter at work in the studio which he shared with Monet, one of whose snow scenes hangs on the wall. Musée du Louvre, Paris.

recognition and no longer needed it.

Renoir did, however, have one devoted critic in his brother Edmond, an aspiring writer who became managing editor of a newspaper, *La Vie Moderne*, started by the distinguished publisher Charpentier. Renoir had painted Charpentier's mother in 1869, and the family were well disposed towards him and his friends. Charpentier, having bought Renoir's *Fisherman on a River Bank* for 180 francs, invited the painter to his house, where such writers as Zola, Maupassant and the Goncourt brothers were welcome guests. Renoir was charmed by the household, and delightedly painted the young daughters who, he said, reminded him of Fragonard. 'I was able to forget the journalists' abuse. I had not only free models but obliging ones.' Edmond, with access to Charpentier's newspaper, wrote several articles in support of the Impressionist painters, his brother in particular. One of these, written in 1879, gives an account of Renoir's methods as a painter. To Renoir, wrote Edmond, the forests of Fontainebleau were better than the four walls of a studio. 'Atmosphere and surroundings had an enormous influence on him. Having no memory of the kind of servitude to which artists so often bind themselves, he let himself be set in motion by his subjects, and above all by the character of the place he was in.' He continued:

'That is the particular quality of his work: he re-stated it everywhere and at all times, from *Lise*, painted in the forest, to the portrait of *Mme Charpentier and her Children*, which was painted in her home without the furniture being moved from its normal daily position, and without anything being prepared to give more importance to one part of the picture than another. When he painted the *Moulin de la Galette* he settled down to it for six months, wedded to this whole world which so enchanted him, and for which models in poses were not good enough. Immersing himself in this whirlpool of pleasure-seeking, he captured the hectic moment with dazzling vivacity. When he painted a portrait he asked his sitter to keep his ordinary clothes, to sit as he always did in his usual position, so that nothing should look uncomfortable or prepared....

'In following my brother's whole output one realizes there is no "method". In none of his works does one find the same way of procedure, yet they hold together all the way through by aiming not at perfection of surface, but at complete understanding of natural harmony.'

Renoir's total refusal to be bound by systems and methods, particularly those urged on him by others, is an essential element in his work. When the painter Laporte told him, 'You must force yourself to draw,' Renoir replied: 'I am like a little cork thrown into the water and carried by the current. I let myself paint as it comes to me.' Gleyre, his teacher, examining a sketch Renoir was working on, said: 'Young man, you are very skilful, very gifted. But no doubt you took up painting just to amuse yourself.' Renoir replied: 'Certainly. If it didn't amuse me I wouldn't be doing it.' Degas, who had a lifelong respect for form, regarded Renoir as a law unto himself: 'He can do anything he likes.'

Renoir. *Lise with a Parasol*, 1867. An early figure study, one of Renoir's first open-air figure subjects, exhibited at the Salon in 1868. Museum Folkwang, Essen.

Renoir. *Figures in a Garden* (date unknown). Poor health, and the rigours of arthritis, obliged Renoir to move south to the Mediterranean coast in 1903. Light and warmth permeate the work of his later years. Ashmolean Museum, Oxford.

Renoir did not exhibit with the Impressionists in 1879 and 1881. Instead he began to travel, first to Algeria for six months, then to Guernsey, and in 1881 to Italy with his young bride Aline Charigot. The experience of Italy impressed and unsettled him. Was Impressionism, after all, a satisfactory end in itself? A painter friend of his with similar doubts, Paul Cézanne, seemed to think not. In 1883 Renoir decided that his art must take another direction. 'I had come to the end of Impressionism, and had arrived at a situation in which I did not know how to paint or draw,' he confessed later. After a period of introspection and experiment he visited Spain in 1886, though briefly, because, as he said: 'When you have seen Velazquez you lose all desire to paint. You realize everything has already been said.'

From now on his style broadened into the loose, flowing, sensuous manner for which he is probably best known: the period of the great nudes and of his glorification of life and Nature. By then the other Impressionists had broken up, the impulse which had held them together having all but died out. Renoir entered into an honoured and productive old age, working to the last with brushes taped to his arthritic hands.

Though he was not one of the Impressionist intellectuals, he took a serious view of his work and method, and understood from his own observations the components of colour laid on canvas. In painting, as in the other arts, he declared in his old age to the art dealer Vollard that not one procedure could be contained in a formula. 'I have wanted to measure out once and for all the oil to be put in my colour. I couldn't do it: I've had to judge it afresh every time. I believe I knew a long time

Above:
Renoir. *Parisiennes Dressed as Algerians*, 1872.
Prompted by his enthusiasm for Delacroix, Renoir visited Algiers in search of exotic themes. His mistress, Lise, was the model. National Museum of Western Art, Tokyo.

Left:
Renoir. *Spring Landscape*, 1877. Impressionism at its most extreme: the forms are dissipated in a hectic shower of coloured lights. Musée National des Beaux-Arts, Algiers.

43

before the "Scientifics" that it is the opposition of yellow and blue that provokes violet shadows. But when you know that, you are still in ignorance of everything. There is a lot to painting that can't be explained and which is essential. You arrive in front of Nature with theories, and Nature throws them to the ground.'

In his last years Renoir was a recognized master, and it was the dealer's business to insist that his work was better than ever. Walter Sickert, one of the leading English followers in the Impressionist mould, protested that 'this transparent flattery combines derision of his intelligence with obvious insult to his masterpieces. . . . Renoir at his best has all the qualities that constitute a great painter, pressed down and running over.' He died at Cagnes on 3 December 1919.

Renoir. *Landscape at Cagnes*, c. 1902. Private Collection. Renoir. *Sailing Boats at Cagnes*, c. 1895. Private Collection.

In his last years, Renoir painted in a mood of domestic contentment. 'You arrive in front of Nature with theories, and Nature throws them to the ground.'

Pissarro

Pissarro. *Self-portrait*, 1873. Musée du Louvre, Paris.

Every movement needs its theorist, a dedicated intelligence to give it continuity and direction. For the Impressionists this function was embodied in Camille Pissarro. He was older than any of them, and in speech and manner the most grave. His seniority gave him an authority which the younger men respected, even if, like them, he had to struggle to make ends meet. Though a convinced anarchist, who believed that the freedom of the artist is indivisible from the freedom of man, he was peaceable and sweet-tempered.

Pissarro was born in the Virgin Islands, the son of a Jewish-French shopkeeper of Spanish or Portuguese descent who sent him to be educated in Paris. There he decided to be a painter and after some exotic wanderings returned to Paris to enrol at the École des Beaux-Arts and the Académie Suisse. The Great Exhibition of 1855 opened his eyes to Corot, Daubigny and Courbet, who between them influenced his early land-scapes. He was accepted at the Salon throughout the 1860s without, however, making much headway with the critics. One of them, comment-ing on his *Banks of the Marne in Winter*, exhibited in 1866, called the

Pissarro. *View of Pontoise, Quai Pothuis*, 1882–3. Pontoise, where Pissarro lived for much of his working life, was a source of numerous subjects, both in the little town and along the banks of the Oise. Städtische Kunsthalle, Mannheim.

Pissarro. *Grey Day on the Banks of the Oise*, 1878.
The subdued tones of Pissarro's palette enabled him to achieve natural effects without resorting to strong colour. Musée du Louvre, Paris.

treatment 'ugly and vulgar' and suggested that the artist was trying to be satirical. As Pissarro's style moved further from the Corot-esque, so his unsold pictures piled up; and as a father with other mouths to feed (he was living with a young woman who had been his mother's maid) he was forced to take odd jobs to earn money.

In these harsh times he made friends with the young men who were to share the adventure ahead. He met Monet in 1861, and a nervous youth from Provence, sorely teased by the others, named Cézanne, who never forgot Pissarro's support for him at the beginning of his career. Cézanne introduced him to Guillaumin and Zola, and through Monet he met Renoir, Sisley and Bazille, who were students together at Gleyre's. With them, Pissarro signed a petition for a new Salon des Refusés after he and the rest of the group were rejected by the Salon in 1867. He shared their pleasure in the rural suburbs around Paris, notably Pontoise and Louveciennes, where his landscapes brightened and grew. Their chief characteristic is a modest subservience to the scenery, rather than an attempt to re-work it into other forms. Like Sisley, he preferred the quiet river banks, winding lanes and rustling fields of the region to the pleasures of city life, an attitude derived, in part, from Millet and the Barbizon painters, with their direct and unliterary view of nature.

Like Monet, in 1870, he fled to England where he had a half-sister. While he was there he heard that his little house in Louveciennes had been used by the besieging Prussians as a butchery. Worse than that, his store of paintings had been put to use as duckboards in the muddy

Pissarro. *The Haystack, Pontoise,* 1873.
In the 1870s a stronger naturalism appeared in Pissarro's work, of which *The Haystack* is an outstanding example. Collection Durand-Ruel, Paris.

garden. His meeting with Monet in London, and the encouragement of the good Daubigny, raised his spirits. The experience of exile seems to have hardened his ideas, not least since his enforced companionship with Monet brought him closer to the fold than he had been in Paris. So far he had been trying to work out his own resolutions of style, palette and manner, while relating them to the example of living artists whose work he knew best, notably Corot, Daubigny and Courbet. Years before, Corot had told him: 'You are an artist. The only advice you need is this: study values. We don't see things the same way. You see green, I see grey and blond. But this is no reason for you not to work at values, because they above all are what one feels and experiences, and one can't make good paintings without them.' Now, with Monet at his elbow, Pissarro was better equipped to trust his own eye. He moved towards the simplicity and dignity which distinguish all but a handful of his most characteristic paintings, patiently adhering to the Impressionist attitudes to light, atmosphere, brushwork and paint.

Back in Paris the friends found things deeply depressing, despite the declaration of the new Republic. The same people seemed to be in positions of authority. There was censorship and favouritism, snobbery and reaction, just as before. Though the bourgeoisie seemed to have survived pretty well there was no money about, and little chance of finding patrons. The Salon was more reactionary than ever. Courbet had been fined and sent to prison for his part in the disturbances. Pissarro had lost most of his pictures. Bazille had not come back from the war.

Pissarro now began spending time with Cézanne, whom he had first met ten years before, and helped to lure him away from the thickly masculine, Romantic style of Courbet to the lighter Impressionist manner. Cézanne learned from Pissarro, while painting alongside him on walks in the country north of Paris, the secrets of broken brushstrokes and enveloping light. For the third Impressionist exhibition, in April 1877, Pissarro and his colleagues on the hanging committee gave Cézanne the best positions. Only Pissarro exhibited at every one of the eight Impressionist exhibitions, sticking to the task when his friends wavered or grew bored.

Pissarro. *View from Louveciennes, c.* 1870. National Gallery, London.
Pissarro. *La Côte des Boeufs a l'Hermitage,* 1877. National Gallery, London.

On his return to France in 1871 Pissarro went to live at Louveciennes. He stayed two years before moving back to Pontoise, where he painted the nearby Hermitage.

49

Materially, the years produced little change in Pissarro's fortunes. But he was not without supporters. A well-to-do painter, Gustave Caillebotte, arrived on the scene and began buying Impressionist pictures. Victor Chocquet, a customs inspector, spent every sou he could afford on them. An opera singer, Jean-Baptiste Faure, became an enthusiastic collector. Charpentier, the publisher, also bought several. Durand-Ruel did his best to bring the friends' names to the fore, buying when he could afford to and taking the risk of adding to his swelling unsold stock.

He was one of those dealers, uncommon at any time, who elevate the trade above mere money-making. 'A genuine picture dealer', he said, 'ought to be at the same time an intelligent connoisseur, ready if need be to sacrifice what seem to be his immediate interests to his artistic conviction. He should prefer to fight speculators rather than join in their activities.' Between 1870 and 1875 he organized ten exhibitions in London including paintings by Pissarro, Manet, Monet, Sisley, Renoir and Degas. He was attacked for exhibiting them, and some of his best clients left him in disgust. On returning to Paris after the 1870 war he found the economic situation so bad that he was obliged to stop buying. To meet his bills he had to sell, at a loss, some fine works by Corot, Delacroix, Millet, Rousseau, and other French masters. After gradually restoring his fortunes by careful dealing in the earlier painters, he began buying Impressionist paintings again in 1880.

By 1884 he was in debt to the tune of 1 million francs. 'I would like to be free to go away and live in a desert,' he confessed to Pissarro. Next year he was invited to organize the first Impressionist exhibition in New York. It opened on 10 April 1886: fifty works by Monet, forty-two by Pissarro, thirty-eight by Renoir, thirty-three by Degas, and others by Manet, Boudin, Berthe Morisot and Mary Cassatt. After a slow start and some hostile reviews, business began to pick up. Following a second New York exhibition in 1887, Durand-Ruel opened his own gallery there. By 1890 he was a rich man. By then, too, the tide had turned for most of the painters whom he had supported. 'You must not think Americans are savages,' he once wrote to Fantin-Latour. 'On the contrary, they are less ignorant and conservative than art-lovers in France. . . .'

Over many years Pissarro's output was comparable to that of the other Impressionists: they all worked fast, averaging about one painting a week. Pissarro's records show that he painted forty-three pictures in 1876, fifty-three in 1877, forty in 1878, thirty-four in 1879. The cost of materials was always pressing, obliging the artists to charge according to the size of the canvas rather than quality or content. When they put their unsold pictures up for auction after the third Impressionist exhibition, the average price fetched was 180 francs. Pissarro sold four canvases, ranging from 106 to 230 francs each. He left Pontoise to rent a room in Montmartre, where he hoped he might be able to sell his work direct to collectors and dealers.

After the sixth Impressionist show in 1881, Pissarro spent a summer with Cézanne at Pontoise. The two men's work during these weeks together is very similar in subject. They were joined by Gauguin, escaping from his office, who took up the Impressionist cause with enthusiasm. It was he who organized the seventh Impressionist exhibition – colliding head-on with the tricky Degas in the process. Durand-Ruel proposed a series of one-man shows in the following year, including one for Pissarro in May. It produced nothing for him except compliments from his fellow painters. Degas told Pissarro that he was pleased to see his work becoming more and more pure. Pissarro, however, had doubts about his style: he was much disturbed, he told his son Lucien, by his 'unpolished and rough execution'. He added that he would like to develop a smoother technique, while retaining 'my old fierceness'.

He was doing his best, at this time, to persuade Gauguin to take a more realistic view of the painter's life. Gauguin had quit his job at the bank in order to paint full-time, and was hungry to begin earning money to keep his wife and five children. 'I regard it a waste of time to think only of selling,' Pissarro confided to Lucien. 'One forgets one's art and exaggerates one's value.' Gauguin had no success with his pictures. He tried to comfort himself with the thought that 'an art which disturbs so many old

convictions' could not be expected to be well received. He went to join his
wife in Copenhagen, where she was desperately working to keep the
family together. Pissarro continued to be his confidant and adviser – an
exhausting role, even for one of his philosophical temperament – and
Gauguin never forgot it.

Pissarro's spirits were revived by a new contact: Paul Signac, whom he
met in Guillaumin's studio in 1885. From him he heard of the work of
another young painter, Georges Seurat, who was introducing a scientific
element into painting by the applications of optics. Seurat's method
appealed to Pissarro as a means of breaking free of his own self-doubts.
The two younger men, delighted to have enlisted the Impressionist
warrior in their cause, saw him as the leader of a new movement (neo-
Impressionism) based on a style in which small dots corresponded to the
various elements of painting, to be joined up, or mixed, by the eye of the
spectator. It was a slow, academic process, and involved long hours in the
studio. Pissarro took it up and was able to persuade the *pointillistes* to take
part in the eighth Impressionist exhibition. Pissarro's attempt to seek a
modern synthesis by methods based on science, as he put it to Durand-
Ruel, dismayed the Impressionists. Durand-Ruel did not like it either,
and refused to buy any of Pissarro's paintings in the new manner. On its
first public appearance, Pointillism was derided as cruelly as once
Impressionism had been. The paintings of Seurat, Signac, Pissarro, and
his son Lucien, were hung together in a separate room, dominated by
Seurat's *La Grande Jatte*. To most visitors the four painters, working
in an identical manner, could hardly be told apart, though to a modern

51

Pissarro. *Evening on the Boulevard Montmartre.* National Gallery, London.
Pissarro. *Boulevard Montmartre in the Spring.* Private Collection.

By 1897, when these works were painted, Pissarro had returned to pure Impressionism after his flirtation with the Pointillist ideas of Seurat.

eye Pissarro's style stands out as intrinsically his own. Before long, he recognized the inhibiting nature of the style, and the unsatisfying results he was getting from it. Having tried it for four years, he abandoned it 'to regain what I have lost, not to lose what I have learned'. So saying, he painted over several of his pointillist landscapes and destroyed the rest.

Pissarro's example, and his selfless support of younger painters, including Cézanne, Gauguin and Van Gogh, won for him a special place in the Impressionists' affections. He had to wait until nearly the end of his life for recognition. In 1892 a retrospective exhibition of his work, organized by Durand-Ruel, established him among the great painters of the age. Ten years later, Gauguin paid tribute to his 'extreme artistic will' and his 'essentially intuitive, well-bred air', adding: 'He was one of my masters, and I do not deny him.' Cézanne, a man of sparing eloquence, said: 'Perhaps we all come from Pissarro.' He died of blood poisoning in Paris on 12 November 1903.

Sisley

Sisley. *Place d'Argenteuil*, 1872. The influence of Corot is apparent in Sisley's work. It was the stabilizing factor in his career. Musée du Louvre, Paris.

Alfred Sisley has the distinction of being grouped with Monet and Pissarro as one of the most consistently 'pure' Impressionists. Compared with their work, his may sometimes seem to lack the hard centre which is one of the marks of a master. But he set himself the same standards, and many of his paintings rank among the most successful work produced even by the band of geniuses who befriended him.

He was an Englishman, born in Paris in 1839 and brought up there until he was eighteen, when his family sent him to London to equip himself for a career in business. After four years he persuaded them to let him return to Paris and be a painter. For a few months he was one of the group at Gleyre's which included Monet, Renoir and Bazille, but he soon began to spend most of his time painting in the countryside at Fontainebleau, Marlotte and St. Cloud. He did not, however, cut himself off from the young painters he had met at Gleyre's; he went on several painting excursions with Monet and also worked with both Renoir and Bazille.

During these early years his work shows little of the inventiveness which was already beginning to separate Monet and Renoir, in particular, from the rest of the group. It was not until the 1870s that he achieved the balance between tone and form that distinguishes his best-known work. His father's business having failed after the 1870 war, Sisley was obliged to paint for his living, and once he turned to painting in earnest, his work assumed a noticeably more professional quality.

Until then, Sisley had been content to learn, rather than set off in his own direction, much as Pissarro digested and rejected the realist influences of the time. Sisley hesitated to adopt the manner of the new, young painters, or even that of Courbet and Daubigny, two senior painters who were to be seen as precursors of the Impressionist movement. Sisley, steeped in Corot, related every current style to his. It proved a justified caution, since it gave his work a stability and focus but for which Sisley might have degenerated into a mere Sunday painter, imitative and derivative all his life. Corot was the stabilizing factor in his career, and Sisley never lost sight of that obligation.

As it is, his Salon pictures of 1866, two views of the village of Marlotte, are pitched in the 'safe' area between tradition and innovation. They were the first pictures of Sisley's to be accepted for the Salon, and they succeed more by charm than by effort: beguilingly low tones, enlivened by sudden touches of colour. In Sisley's early work the structure often seems flabby, however well-realized the passages of natural description. The impact of Monet does not appear until 1869, when Sisley seems more ready to leave the studio and work out of doors, motivated perhaps by the sparkling and buoyant paintings which Monet and Renoir, working side by side, made at La Grenouillère that summer.

Sisley was drawn closer into the Impressionist circle through the friends' frequent gatherings at the Café Guerbois, in the Batignolles quarter of Paris, where the company usually included Monet, Renoir, Degas and Manet. Though very different in character and temperament, they were united in what John Rewald, historian and chronicler of the Impressionists and their age, calls 'a common contempt for official art and a determination to seek the truth away from the beaten track'. Since they were nearly all looking for truth in a different direction, the notion of a 'school' does not apply; they were known simply as *le groupe des Batignolles*. There is a painting of them by Fantin-Latour, *A Studio in the Batignolles Quarter*, showing Manet at his easel, with Renoir, described as 'a painter who will get himself talked about'; Astruc, the poet; Émile

Sisley. *The Rest by a Stream at the Edge of a Wood*, 1872. The epitome of Sisley's identification with the deep green peace of rural France. Musée du Louvre, Paris.

Zola; Maître, philosopher and musician; Bazille; Monet; and the German
painter Otto Scholderer. We might wonder why Fantin-Latour left out
Pissarro, already a prominent member of the company, and young Sisley.
Both were among the group with Monet, Renoir and Berthe Morisot, who
tried their luck by putting some of their paintings up for auction at the
Drouot Galleries in 1874 – an occasion which ended in one outraged
spectator calling Berthe Morisot a streetwalker. Pissarro punched the
offender in the face, a brawl started, and someone called the police. Not a
single picture was sold.

Sisley's world is not so much that of the cafés and boulevards as of the
quiet countryside, especially along rivers and water-meadows. His
paintings have an airiness which gives them a distinctive mood, achieved
by his sure touch with both colour and tone. They are undemonstrative
pictures, reflections of a private nature. The lack of documentation in his
life can be partly attributed to his preferred solitariness – though from all
accounts he was vivacious enough in his own home, in a life shared with
his attractive wife, Marie, a Parisienne whose own family seems to have
fallen on hard times. It is tempting to identify her as the girlish figure who
graces several of Sisley's landscapes about 1866.

By degrees, after a conventional start, Sisley found his own style and
palette. Increasingly his free but carefully varied brushwork and feeling
for suffused light, give his best work an air of contained energy, an
undramatic mastery which recalls Corot. Encouraged by his friends, and
by Durand-Ruel who began buying some of his pictures, Sisley strove to
mend his fortunes after the collapse of 1870. To save on expenses, he
moved his home from Paris to the semi-rural suburbs: first to Louveciennes, then to Marly-le-Roi and Sèvres. His favourite painting ground
became the narrow reaches of the Seine with its towpaths, bridges and
tranquil river traffic. His eye for interestingly solid forms – pillars,
bridges, arches, ironwork – led him to subjects which move beyond the

picturesque to the qualities of mass and texture. In 1874, on a visit to England, he painted several versions of the bridge at Hampton Court, then newly built, including one of the structure as seen from underneath. A pair of scullers slide by, dwarfed by the pillars and beams. In the same year he painted the aquaduct at Marly, in which a passing horseman contributes the necessary counterpoint of grace and motion. Some of his last paintings, in the 1890s, return to the observation of light on mass. His oil studies of the church of Notre-Dame, at Moret, show the effect of light on the ancient stones, first in sunshine and then in rain: a response, perhaps, to Monet's paintings of Rouen Cathedral, which he might have had a chance of seeing in his friend's studio.

In the later paintings there is a strengthening of the skies, which, however sombrely painted, remain in Sisley's pictures the source of light. True to his eye, he continued to paint what he saw, not what he knew to be there – an essentially Impressionist principle to which he remained as loyal as the arch-Impressionist, Pissarro. A letter survives in which Sisley explains how a painting can be painted in more than one manner – tiny touches to capture the sparkling quality of light on water, smoother passages for fields and skies. A critic writing at the time, Jules Laforgue, might have been describing Sisley's art when he wrote of the Impressionists' abandoning the 'three supreme illusions' of academic painting: line, perspective and studio lighting. He went on: 'Where the one sees only the external outline of objects, the other – the Impressionist – sees the living lines, not put together geometrically but in a thousand irregular strokes which, seen at a distance, establish life. Where the one sees things placed in perspective planes, according to a theoretical design, the other – the Impressionist again – sees perspective conveyed by a thousand little touches of tone and brush, and by all kinds of atmospheric states.'

By the 1880s, critics were beginning to accept Impressionism on its own terms. Sisley, among the rest, attracted comment as a true innovator in a kind of painting described by a German commentator as 'rendering the fleeting impact which our surroundings make on us. This method leaves out a number of details, and above all tries to capture a whole, a mood, regardless of how incomplete it may seem according to ordinary conceptions.' Of a work by Sisley, a coastline with villas, he added that it was so delicately light and shimmering, so harmonious in composition, that one could find no fault with it. 'Here is no attempt to paint anything which could not at will be made out by the naked eye. The painting achieves its effect by its airy lightness and unique harmony.'

Sisley's work in the last decade of his life shows no sign of strain or degeneration. He moved to a small house, close to the church of Moret, where he continued to entertain any of his friends who might call while he was working. He was delighted by his children, who were friends with Monet's. He made a last visit to the British Isles in 1897, painting at Penarth on the south coast of Wales. The landscape, so different from the

Left:
Sisley. *The Path to the Old Ferry at By*, c. 1880. Tate Gallery, London.

Above:
Sisley. *Cornfield near Argenteuil*, 1873. Argenteuil lay outside the built-up areas of Paris, on the edge of open country. It was a favourite painting-ground of the Impressionists. Hamburger Kunsthalle.

Right:
Sisley. *The Watering-place at Port-Marly*, c. 1875.
There are several versions of this subject, in which Sisley catches the shimmer of water against the solid outlines of posts and walls. National Gallery, London.

Far right:
Sisley. *Small Meadows in Spring*, c. 1885. Sisley shared Pissarro's fondness for riverside scenery along the banks of the Seine or the Oise. The 'small meadows' were near his home at Moret-sur-Loing. Tate Gallery, London.

woods and fields of France, appealed to him nonetheless. He painted his first, and last, seascape. On his return, Marie Sisley, overwhelmed by a strange weakness, languished and died. Sisley was also ill, from cancer. He asked Monet to come and see him, and to look after the children. A week later he died.

Monet helped to organize a sale of the paintings left in Sisley's studio as a means of raising money for his destitute family. Dealers and collectors descended on Sisley's little home at Moret-sur-Loing, near Fontaine-bleau. Everything was sold. Within a year, a painting for which Sisley had once accepted 100 francs was sold for 45,000. It was *The Flood at Port Marly*, one of three versions which Sisley painted of that subject in 1876. It is now in the Louvre.

A week before he died, Pissarro paid Sisley a tribute he would have valued: 'He is a great and beautiful artist – in my opinion, a master equal to the greatest.'

Right:
Sisley. *Boats on the Seine*, c. 1877.
The brushwork matches the breadth and drama of the river, seen as an industrial waterway under a powerful sky.
Courtauld Institute Galleries, London.

Below:
Sisley. *Boat During the Flood, Port-Marly*, c. 1876.
This is probably the version of the flood that was shown at the Impressionist exhibition of 1876.
Musée du Louvre, Paris.

The Aftermath: Cézanne, Gauguin and Van Gogh

For all their struggles and discouragements, the Impressionists succeeded in bringing about a fundamental change in the way painters approached their work. Their vivid use of colour could not be ignored. It influenced other, more conventionally-minded painters, to the point where Émile Zola, their staunchest friend among the writers and critics of the age, thought they had gone too far: 'Was it for this that I fought – those patches of colour, these reflections, this decomposition of light? Was I mad?' On a deeper level, the demonstration that an artist could set off in a direction of his own choosing was more important still. The liberation of light was one thing; the liberation of the painter's process was another. The whole function of painting had been challenged, and new answers suggested to old problems. The idea of 'finish' as essential to a work of art had been contradicted. The sketch was elevated to a position never known before, an object fit for exhibition in its own right, not simply for private satisfaction or as a study for a worked-up painting. This represented a change in aesthetic values which has lasted into the modern age. It helps to explain the enthusiasm with which, in England, John Constable's oil sketches – preliminary exercises for his great 'six-footers' – were newly discovered; and it contributed to the international reassessment of J. M. W. Turner.

Nevertheless, the first flush of Impressionism was already over by the 1880s. The criticisms levelled at it even by friendly commentators, of wilfully slapdash and insubstantial painting, had their effect. Monet expressed himself as no longer satisfied with the quick, outdoor impression, and undertook to introduce what he called 'more serious qualities'. Even Pissarro, the guardian of the Impressionist conscience, admitted in the end that 'the unity which the human spirit gives to vision' could only be found in the studio, the place – in Pissarro's mature view – where a painter's previously scattered impressions are co-ordinated in a

Cézanne. *Still Life with Fruit Basket, c.* 1888–90. A new commitment to solid form gives Cézanne's still-life paintings and watercolours a startling freshness. Musée du Louvre, Paris.

work of art. In short, by the end of the nineteenth century there was a readiness among thoughtful painters to go back to the true sources of painterly ideas, while acknowledging the revolutionary benefits of the Impressionist achievement.

In particular, three painters of genius emerged, overlapping the Impressionists in time and manner, whose names have become synonymous with the post-Impressionist movement: Cézanne, Gauguin and Van Gogh. Between them they set European painting on a path which turned Impressionism into something solid and durable, like the art of the museums – a return, in effect, to the mainstream, but with minds alight with discovery and purpose.

Cézanne had shown two paintings in the first Impressionist exhibition of 1874. The first showed a woman half crouching, half sprawling on a bed, her nudity abruptly exposed by an apparently naked negress plucking back the coverlet while a clothed and bearded onlooker gazed up at her from a deep divan. It was called *A Modern Olympia*, an obvious derivation from Manet's notorious exhibit in the Salon of 1865. The other was a painting executed largely with a palette knife, of a house and farm buildings bathed in soft, golden sunlight, called *The House of the Hanged Man*. Each, in its degree, forced itself on the spectator: the *Olympia* with its eroticism, its distortions, and its violent, slapdash colours; and the landscape with its fierce honesty of tone and composition. The critic of the journal *L'Artiste*, while letting Monet, Renoir and Degas off lightly, called the *Olympia* 'a nightmare' and Cézanne a 'bit of a madman, afflicted with painting delirium tremens', adding: 'No audacity can surprise us. But when it comes to landscapes M. Cézanne will allow us to pass in silence over his *House of the Hanged Man....*'

Cézanne can hardly have been surprised, or unduly disappointed. For years he had been trying to get accepted at the Salon, though his chances

Cézanne. *The Bay of
Marseilles Seen from
L'Estaque*, 1882–5.
Musée du Louvre,
Paris.
Cézanne. *L'Estaque:
The Village and Sea*,
1879–83.
Private Collection.

The struggle to find a
way back to basic
painting culminated in
Cézanne's
rediscovery of mass,
touching on
abstraction.

were not improved by his habit of trundling his work round in a barrow, dressed like a hawker, to demonstrate his contempt for the whole proceedings. The *Modern Olympia*, even to a twentieth-century eye, seems almost wilfully provocative: a sardonic jest, a *jeu d'esprit* with a sting in it. *The House of the Hanged Man*, though considerably less outrageous in subject, lumped Cézanne with Pissarro and Monet. (It found a buyer, however: Victor Chocquet, a lowly customs official who had already begun to buy Impressionist paintings.) Taken together, the two works sum up the kind of painter Cézanne already was, and the fervent, contradictory nature which was to lead him, in the end, to greatness.

He came from Aix-en-Provence, the son of a self-made businessman who graduated from money-lending to banking, a demanding, overbearing parent whom Cézanne respected and dreaded all his life. He expected his son to make his way in the new-rich world of the bourgeoisie, preferably as a lawyer, but eventually agreed to let him try his hand at being a painter. Cézanne came to Paris and conscientiously attended life classes at the Académie Suisse, at the same time acquainting himself with the masters in the Louvre. He was neither fluent nor easily satisfied, and his frustrations drove him to outbursts of passion which disconcerted his friends. Of these, Émile Zola, who had known him from their schooldays, predicted that, though Cézanne might have the makings of a great painter, 'he will never have the genius to become one. The least obstacle makes him despair.'

Cézanne. *Bather Diving into the Water*, 1867–70.
The male nude became an instrument of Cézanne's explorations of weight and space. National Museum of Wales, Cardiff.

Cézanne's brooding nature set a distance between him and other men, even those who felt nothing but respect for him. Though he worked closely with the Impressionists for some five years, and especially with Pissarro, he never acquired their dexterity. This was due in equal parts to his own views on painting, which diverged from theirs at several points, and to his method of work, which was as slow and tortured as theirs was deft and vivacious. Rilke, the German poet, has left a vivid pen-picture describing how Cézanne 'gave himself entirely, his whole strength behind each stroke of the brush. You only needed to see him at work, painfully tense, his face as if in prayer, to realize how much spirit went into the task. He would shake all over, his face heavy with unseen thoughts, his chest sunken, his shoulders hunched, his hands trembling until the moment came. Then, firm and fast, they began to work gently, always from right to left, with a will of their own.'

Cézanne himself, when he was nearly seventy, wrote to the painter Émile Bernard: 'The main line to follow is just to put down what you see. Never mind your temperament or your ability in respect of Nature.... Those outlines done in black are quite mistaken. The answer lies in consulting Nature; that is where we find the means.' On the face of it, those are Impressionist sentiments. But Cézanne was not a man to identify himself with any particular school or set of rules. He interpreted the lessons taught him by Pissarro ('the humble and colossal Pissarro' as he called him) in his own way. Colour could produce form, but form must be more than one-dimensional. Short brushstrokes could bring life to inanimate objects, but short brushstrokes applied in parallel diagonals could bring rhythm and unity. Colours laid side by side could achieve brilliant, vibrating tones, but colours in which one plane falls on top of another contribute solidity and structure. In Cézanne's work, colour does not dissolve shapes – it gives them weight and form. The consideration given to each touch was agonizing; and between each one he would carefully clean his brush. All this gives his paintings a deep-rooted quality which harks back to the greatest masters, dismissing the accretions of centuries and stripping the painter's art to its essentials.

Cézanne's purposes were as severe as his methods. In his exploration of the painter's true function he confined himself, in the twenty years of his full maturity, to relatively simple images. He distrusted the element of decoration which he saw in the Impressionists, and was totally disinterested in the sort of subjects which delighted them: the gaiety and humanity of everyday life. His dictum 'Just put down what you see' meant something different to him, since he put his eyes to different use. He was looking for the form which underlies natural objects – he even called his paintings 'constructions after nature'. To see things as they really are he sought to divest them of all literary and sentimental associations. He was as incapable of introducing an element of ingratiation into a picture as into a personal relationship.

The lack of such easy communication makes his work less 'popular' than that of the Impressionists, but he foresaw that this would be so. After exhibiting with the Impressionists again in 1877 he withdrew to Aix and all but vanished from the metropolitan scene. Renoir and Monet sometimes visited him and brought back stories of the self-inflicted rigours of his life and work. In 1886 Cézanne came into his inheritance when his father died (he and his two sisters shared a fortune of 2 million francs) but it seemed to mean nothing to him. He continued to tramp the fields looking for subjects, destroying countless paintings and sketches in sudden rages, or discarding them among rocks, frightening off visitors, alternating between excitement and despair.

In 1895 the dealer Ambroise Vollard, encouraged by Pissarro for whom Cézanne assumed the stature of a master, decided to hold a retrospective exhibition of his works in Paris. Nobody at the time seemed to know where Cézanne was living. Vollard tracked him down, though with difficulty, and Cézanne obligingly sent him 150 rolled-up canvases. When the exhibition opened in November it made a powerful impact, not so much on the public as on the leading painters of the day. Pissarro wrote to his son Lucien: 'My enthusiasm is nothing compared with Renoir's. Even Degas has succumbed to the charm of this refined savage. Monet, all of us — were we wrong?'

Cézanne. *The Card Players*, c. 1893. The Impressionist liberation of the palette is used by Cézanne to create a living presence within a strong design. Courtauld Institute Galleries, London.

Gauguin's arrival on the scene could hardly have been better timed. Impressionism, having to all appearances led nowhere in particular, was threatened by an increasing appetite in intellectual and literary circles for theosophical notions of the one-ness of art, life and sensations, and the search for metaphors in which these ideas could be expressed. The Impressionists' demonstration that truth can be captured in a glance began to look insubstantial, even if their paintings were by now beginning to be understood and, increasingly, enjoyed. Gauguin was both steeped in the Impressionists (he had his own collection of their works) and resistant to the idea that what matters in art is the sensation activated by the painter's eye. For him, as for Cézanne, the painter's function went deeper, into what he called 'the mysterious centre of the mind'.

The story of his life has become a fable, and hardly needs re-telling. After twelve years of marriage and well-paid servitude in a stockbroker's office, he abandoned his wife, children and career to become a full-time painter. He was drawn particularly to Pissarro, with whom he went painting in Pontoise, which led to his exhibiting in the Impressionist exhibitions of 1880, 1882 and 1886. Then came his move to Pont-Aven in Britanny, where he became the focus of a movement dedicated to non-naturalistic and symbolic art. He started to paint in flat, broad areas of

Gauguin. *Vahine note Tiare*, 1891.
The primitivism which Gauguin admired in his Tahitian models introduced a new element into European art. Ny Carlsberg Glyptotek, Copenhagen.

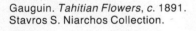

Gauguin. *Tahitian Flowers*, c. 1891.
Stavros S. Niarchos Collection.

Gauguin. *Breton Landscape: The Mill*, 1894. 'One bit of advice', wrote Gauguin to another painter. 'Don't copy nature too much. Art is an abstraction.' Musée du Louvre, Paris.

colour. 'Work madly and freely,' he told his group, 'and you will make progress. Above all, don't labour over your picture. A great emotion can be translated immediately. Dream over it, and look for the simplest form.' These ideas and methods were further developed in his well-known Tahitian paintings which marked the end of his Impressionist years.

The themes, colours and constructions of Gauguin's later work, by which he is best known, tend to overshadow the Impressionistic borrowings of his work in the 1880s. By then most of the group were moving away from the early innocence of the Impressionist vision. Monet's style had assumed a roughness of structure and technique; Degas was engrossed in his pastels of women at their private rituals (he never exhibited publicly after 1886); Renoir was showing a renewed concern for detail and a less mellifluous pigment; Cézanne was working out his notions of weight and form. If Gauguin looked back to the beginnings of the revolution, it was to Manet's *Olympia*, which he copied in 1891. To him, and to Van Gogh, it was time to move on.

Gauguin disliked suggestions that Cézanne and Van Gogh were the effectual leaders of the Post-Impressionist movement, or that his own style owed a debt either to them or to his immediate predecessors. Nevertheless, it is a fact that he emerged at a time when the struggle to establish new principles and new aesthetics in painting was beginning to show results. Gauguin died in May 1903, on the island of his self-imposed exile. In October of that year a vivid summary of his achievement appeared in the review *L'Orient*, written by the painter Maurice Denis. Gauguin, Denis wrote, was 'the unquestioned master who won our admiration by his talent, his fluency, his gestures, his physical strength, his harshness, his inexhaustible imagination, his very strong head for drink, his romantic bearing.... He wanted to convey character, to express the "inner idea" even in what was ugly.

'But the Impressionist idea was by no means obsolete. We could subsist on what we had learned from Renoir or Degas. Gauguin transmitted their lessons to us, enriched what he had himself borrowed from the classical traditions and from Cézanne. He revealed Cézanne's achievement to us, not as that of an independent genius, an irregular follower of Manet, but as what it really is: the end product of long exertion, the necessary result of a great crisis.'

Impressionism in Gauguin still meant sunshine, diffused light, freedom of composition, the sense of the outdoors revealed by Corot, a shimmering technique, the love of bright colour, and the influence of Japanese art. Gauguin gave artists 'the right to lyricism', to exaggerate those impressions which justify the metaphors of poetry.

Van Gogh. *Restaurant de la Sirène, Joinville*, 1887. Musée du Louvre, Paris.

Van Gogh entered the world of the Impressionists in 1886, when he was thirty-six. Behind him lay the experiences of an artist struggling for expression: first in Paris, then England, then back in Holland to study for the Church, followed by missionary work among the coalminers of the Borinage district of Belgium. Dismissed from the mission for 'excess of zeal' (he went about in home-made clothes, slept on the ground in a wooden hut and gave all he had to the local poor), he wandered from Brussels to The Hague and from The Hague to Antwerp, teaching himself to paint and draw. In 1886 he joined his brother Theo, who ran an art gallery in Paris devoted to living artists, and it was there that he discovered the Impressionists.

Until then, Van Gogh had known only the Dutch painters and a handful of French landscape painters, including Millet and the Barbizon group. Now, for the first time, he saw works by Delacroix (whom he later said had more effect on him than the Impressionists) and by Pissarro, Cézanne, Renoir and Sisley. Light, colour and brilliance burst upon him. He went about the streets and cafés with a palette of bright colours, as delighted by the cosmopolitan bustle of the city as Manet, Monet, Renoir and the others had been twenty years before. He met Pissarro, who was then moving towards the pointillist technique of Seurat, a painter who excited Van Gogh perhaps more than any of his contemporaries at this time. It was Pissarro who uttered the famous dictum that, the moment he laid eyes on Van Gogh, 'I knew he would either go mad or surpass us all. But I did not know he would do both.'

Van Gogh. *The Church at Auvers-sur-Oise*,
1890.
This painting belongs to the last weeks of Van
Gogh's life, when he was lodging at Auvers
under the care of Dr. Paul Gachet. Musée du
Louvre, Paris.

In Antwerp, Van Gogh had not even known who the Impressionists
were. Now he wrote in a letter to the English painter, Henry Livens: 'I
have seen them, and though not being one of their club yet I have much
admired certain Impressionist pictures – Degas' nude figures, a Claude
Monet landscape.' Through the young Toulouse-Lautrec he was brought
in touch with members of the avant-garde of the art world, and with the
café society where Lautrec felt most at home. Van Gogh succumbed to
the pleasures of an artist's life in Paris. He wrote to his sister: 'I still go on
having the most impossible, and not very seemly, love affairs from which
I emerge as a rule damaged and shamed and little else.' Perhaps the
woman at the 'Tambourin' was one of those who momentarily became
part of his life: Toulouse-Lautrec painted her, too, in an identical pose, as
Poudre-de-riz ('face powder'). Another discovery was Japanese art, then at
the height of its popularity. The Impressionists were enthusiastic for
Japanese prints, printed in clear flat colours akin to their own ideas of
colour and design. Van Gogh pinned them on his walls, and they appear
in the backgrounds of some of his paintings.

This combination of influences, and the stimulus of sympathetic
friends, for a time gave him new hope. But it was not long before Van
Gogh grew tired of Paris. The strain of city life exhausted and depressed
him, and he yearned for the sun. Toulouse-Lautrec recommended
Provence. One evening, as if on an impulse, Van Gogh decided to leave,
but not before preparing the studio so that his brother Theo would think
he was still at home. He put a canvas on the easel and piled other

paintings around the walls. Then he left for Arles in the south of France, and the splendours and miseries waiting for him there.

Between February 1888 and his death by suicide eighteen months later, Van Gogh painted his greatest pictures, an achievement which, for concentrated genius, has no parallel in the history of art. Drawing on his accumulated knowledge and experience, he at once entered into his own world. By setting certain colours side by side he achieved effects of ringing splendour. To colour he brought dignity and form, the opposite of the abstractions into which Monet was heading and which seemed the inevitable limit of Impressionist techniques.

Here can be seen the outline and justification for the art which was to follow, in which intuitive and subconscious response to themes, shapes and forms were to give painters total emancipation even from their traditional materials. Cézanne, Gauguin and Van Gogh in their different ways carried Western painting into the twentieth century: Cézanne by insisting on the conceptual value of things seen, rather than simply on what strikes the eye; Gauguin by releasing the power of primitive images and symbols; and Van Gogh by the revelation of colour as a means of expressing the most intense responses of the human spirit.

No doubt, in the sum of things, these were to prove more substantial than even the achievements of the Impressionists, if only because most great truths cannot be captured in a glance, however brilliantly perceptive. Even so, Impressionism marks a turning point in the history of Western art. It is still with us, still capable of invoking beauty and surprise, still communicating its unique blend of poignancy and pleasure.

Van Gogh. *Peach Trees in Blossom*, 1889.
One of a series of landscapes painted at Arles in April, when the fruit trees were in bloom. Courtauld Institute Galleries, London.

The Impressionists' Circle

Baudelaire, Charles

In addition to his remarkable work as a poet, Baudelaire – born 21 April 1821 – was a critic of great discernment. His reviews of the Salon exhibitions reflect his impatience with the mediocrity that the Impressionists were to challenge. An admirer of Delacroix, a champion of Constantin Guys and of Daumier, he recognized Manet's 'taste for modern truth'. In 1862 Manet made a witty etching of Baudelaire in profile, which he included in his *Concert in the Tuileries Gardens*, one of his formative early studies of everyday life. Baudelaire died on 31 August 1867.

Bazille, Jean-Frédéric

Born at Montpelier on 6 December 1841, the son of a professional family who wanted him to become a doctor. He broke off his medical studies to start painting in Paris, entering Gleyre's studio in 1862 where he met Monet, Renoir and Sisley. He shared lodgings with Renoir, whom he subsidized from his allowance, and every summer returned to Montpelier to paint. The most obvious influence on his style is Manet. In 1867 he bought a painting from Monet's studio, *Women in the Garden*, for which he gave 2,500 francs, payable in monthly instalments. A popular member of the Café Guerbois set, he appears in Manet's *Déjeuner sur l'Herbe* and in Fantin-Latour's *The Studio at Batignolles*. At the outbreak of the Franco-Prussian war in 1870 he enlisted in the Zouaves, and was killed in action on 28 November the same year.

Boudin, Eugène-Louis

Born at Honfleur on 12 July 1824, the son of a ship's captain. Boudin began painting in his twenties and was awarded a grant to study in Paris. Strongly influenced by Corot, he exhibited at the Salon in 1859. His encounter with the youthful Monet encouraged the boy to start painting

Seurat. *The Circus*, 1891.
The 'scientific' element in Pointillism, perfected by Seurat, carried Impressionism down another path. Musée du Louvre, Paris.

Right:
Boudin. *Laundresses by a Stream*, 1885.
Although Boudin was not a member of the Impressionists' circle, his style shows signs of their influence. National Gallery, London.

open-air scenes. Like Monet, he also learned from Jongkind, who painted in Normandy and along the Channel coast. Boudin's bright palette and breezy style bring him close to the Impressionists, with whom he exhibited as a token of support at the first of their exhibitions in 1874. He never formally joined them, but was a kindred spirit until his death in Deauville on 8 August 1898.

Cassatt, Mary

Born in 1845, the daughter of a Pennsylvanian banker of French ancestry. She spent her schooldays in France and subsequently travelled in Europe before settling in Paris, where she exhibited in the Salons of 1872 and 1874. Degas showed an interest in her work and the two became close. As his model she figures in several of Degas' works. She aligned herself with the Impressionists and exhibited with them four times between 1879 and 1886. Mary Cassatt was largely instrumental, through her access to well-placed Americans, in securing recognition for the Impressionists in the United States. She died at Beauvais on 19 June 1926.

Caillebotte, Gustave

A painter, born in 1848, who was close to the Impressionists and exhibited with them in five of their exhibitions between 1876 to 1882. As well as painting, he collected his friends' pictures, which he intended should pass to the French state on his death. The bequest consisted of no less than sixty-five works, including eight by Renoir, sixteen by Monet, five by Cézanne, seven by Degas. When Caillebotte died in 1894 they were officially rejected, in terms of outrage and contempt. Renoir, executor of the will, was forced to weed out the paintings to which the authorities most violently objected – well over half. Only in 1928 was the entire collection admitted to the Louvre.

Cézanne, Paul

Born at Aix-en-Provence on 19 January 1839, the son of a self-made businessman in the town who intended him for the law. Cézanne left for Paris to study painting in 1861, failed the entrance examinations of the École des Beaux-Arts and joined the Académie Suisse. There he met Pissarro, and soon became a member of *la bande à Manet*. Pissarro's support and advice helped to keep him at work, but he exhibited with the Impressionists only twice: in the first show, and in 1877. Thereafter he went his own way, to become the most influential painter of his time, an old master in a modern age. He died at Aix on 22 October 1906.

Chocquet, Victor

Born in 1821, Chocquet entered the Impressionist circle in 1875 when he attended the auction at the Hôtel Drouot of works by Renoir, Monet, Sisley and Berthe Morisot, which the group had organized in a desperate effort to make some sales. A customs official with only his modest salary to spend on collecting, he already owned a number of pictures by Delacroix. He met Renoir and asked if he would paint his wife, with one of his Delacroix paintings in the background. Renoir took a liking to him, performed the commission and subsequently painted two portraits of Chocquet himself. Renoir introduced him to Cézanne's work, and Chocquet at once became an enthusiastic supporter. He next met Monet, whose work he also began to collect. He died in 1891 and his widow inherited his collection. When it was sold after her death it included thirty-five Cézannes, twelve Monets, fourteen Renoirs, five Manets and one painting each by Sisley and Pissarro.

Corot, Jean-Baptist Camille

Born in Paris on 16 July 1796. After training as a conventional landscape painter he took to sketching out of doors, developing his own style of lyrical romanticism. The freshness and directness of his work put him alongside Constable, whose painting *The Hay Wain* he might have seen at the Salon of 1824, when Bonington also exhibited there. Boudin and the young Impressionists respected him for seeking his subjects, as they did, in the open air, though he preferred to finish them in the studio. Pissarro

Cassatt. *Mother and Child.*
As an American painter, Mary Cassatt helped to bring the Impressionists' work to the notice of transatlantic collectors. Musée du Louvre, Paris.

Corot. *The Bridge at Narni*, 1826–7. Musée du Louvre, Paris.

had more to do with him than the other members of the group, except perhaps Berthe Morisot, whom Corot particularly liked and encouraged. He died on 22 February 1875.

Couture, Thomas
An historical and portrait painter, born in 1815. A pupil of Gros, he owes his place in art history to the fact that he gave lessons to Manet, Fantin-Latour and Puvis de Chavannes. He died in 1879.

Daubigny. *Landscape with Cattle by a Stream*, 1872. Though not a precursor of Impressionism, Daubigny's encouragement and example made a valuable contribution to the Impressionists' early days. National Gallery, London.

Daubigny, Charles-François
Born on 15 February 1817, the son of a landscape artist. Daubigny found himself as a painter when he started working in the Barbizon manner, largely out of doors. His riverside scenes and tranquil landscapes were accepted at the Salon, but he had great sympathy with the Impressionists – all younger painters – and their aims. He was particularly helpful to Pissarro and Monet when he met them, as a fellow refugee, in London after the Franco-Prussian war. He died on 19 February 1878.

Degas, Hilaire-Germain Edgar

Born on 19 June 1834, into a prosperous banking family. Enrolled at the École des Beaux-Arts in 1855 and learned the qualities of draughtsmanship from Ingres. A feeling for realism of the kind introduced by the camera, and an eye for quick, journalistic compositions, give his work a startling modernity. An early friend of the Impressionists, and a co-exhibitor, he moved away from them as his career progressed. His masterly drawings, paintings and sculptures of figure subjects, caught with an unerring eye for natural movement and gesture, are lasting contributions to European art. He died on 27 September 1917.

Denis, Maurice

Born in Granville in 1870, one of the generation of French painters whose careers began in the wake of Impressionism. In 1901 he painted his *Homage to Cézanne*, a large canvas which was exhibited at the Salon, showing a group of artists – Redon, Vuillard, Bonnard and Denis himself – gathered around a still-life by Cézanne. Denis became a leading Symbolist painter and exponent of modern art theory. He died in 1943.

Durand-Ruel, Paul

A picture dealer, born in 1831, who began by buying works of the Barbizon painters and also supported Courbet. He took an interest in the Impressionists from their earliest appearances and bought their work, notably twenty-three paintings from Manet's studio in 1872, for which he paid 35,000 francs. At an exhibition which he arranged in London the same year, he showed thirteen Manets, nine Pissarros, three works by Degas, four by Monet and three by Degas – with an almost total lack of success. He had better fortune in Paris the following year, but the market then went into a deep depression and he came close to bankruptcy. Salvation came from America, where after an uncertain and hostile start the Impressionists began to find patrons. He died, prosperous and vindicated, in 1922.

Fantin-Latour, Ignace-Henri Jean Théodore

Born at Grenoble on 14 January 1836. He was taught by his father and in Courbet's studio. An early champion of Manet, and a member of the Café Guerbois circle, he exhibited at the Salon des Refusés in 1863 but never attached himself to the Impressionist movement. His flower studies are his most admired contributions to the art of his time. He died on 25 August 1904.

Fantin-Latour. *Roses*, 1890. National Gallery, London.

Fisher, Mark

Born in Boston, Massachusetts in 1841. He studied at Gleyre's atelier in Paris from 1863, where he was a contemporary of Sisley, Monet and Bazille. Pissarro called him 'the first of our imitators'. He came to England in 1872, married and settled in London, where he quickly achieved a reputation. A number of Fishers were included in the famous collection of Impressionist paintings bought by the dealer Hugh Lane, which are now in Dublin. He died in April 1923.

Gleyre, Charles

A painter and teacher, in whose atelier Renoir, Sisley, Monet, Whistler and Bazille studied in their early days. The tuition included painting from the nude from 8 a.m. to 12 a.m. every day except Sunday, and for two hours every afternoon except Saturday. The pupils were of all ages, talents and temperaments, and discipline was minimal. Gleyre disliked lecturing, and seldom corrected the students' work, leaving them, as Renoir said, pretty much to their own devices. He placed great emphasis on drawing, usually at the expense of colour. To one student who ventured to use a certain red in his picture, Gleyre exclaimed: 'Be careful not to become another Delacroix!'

Gonzalès, Eva

Manet's only pupil, whom he met in 1863, when she was twenty and taking instruction from Chaplin. Manet asked her to sit for him, and exhibited the resulting painting at the Salon of 1870, where she too had a painting accepted, very much in Manet's style. In 1878 she married the engraver, Henri Guérard. The death of Manet on 5 May 1883, occurred just after she had given birth to a baby. Two days after the funeral, she died of an embolism.

Guillaumin, Armand
Born at Moulins in 1841, Guillaumin is a less familiar figure than the other Impressionists, but he was an active and accomplished member of their circle. He was at the Académie Suisse with Pissarro and Cézanne, and later worked as a clerk in the municipal offices and as a ditch-digger to finance his painting. In 1891 he had the good fortune to win 100,000 francs in the city lottery. He died in Paris in 1927, having in his time worked with the leading painters of the age, from Pissarro and Cézanne to Signac and Van Gogh.

Guillaumin. *Sunset at Ivry, c.* 1873.
One of the less prominent members of the Impressionist group, Guillaumin was faithful to their principles all his life. Musée du Louvre, Paris.

Left:
Manet. *Portrait of Eva Gonzalès*, 1870.
A pupil of Manet, whom she met in 1869, Eva Gonzalès exhibited at the Salon the following year. National Gallery, London.

Gauguin, Paul

Born on 4 June 1848, the son of a journalist. As a youth, Gauguin first went to sea then into a stockbroker's office. He married, began to do well in his job, then threw it all up to be a painter. He attached himself to Pissarro at Pontoise and showed with the Impressionists at their exhibitions in 1880, 1881, 1882 and 1886. His move to Pont-Aven, Brittany, led him to the symbolism which was his point of departure from the Impressionist idea. His exposure to the genius of Van Gogh, whom he stayed with at Arles, left its mark. His South Seas paintings set the seal on a life of explosive achievement. He died at Atuana, in the Marquesas Islands, on 8 May 1903.

Jongkind, Johan-Berthold

A Dutchman, born near Rotterdam on 3 June 1819. Jongkind trained as a landscape painter and moved to Paris in 1846. There he met Eugène Isabey, a painter of watercolour landscapes and marine subjects, who introduced him to the Normandy coast. Jongkind exhibited at the Salon des Refusés in Paris in 1863 and made an impact on the Impressionists, who recognized in his quick, direct style an approach to painting that was close to their own. He died on 19 February 1891.

Manet, Edouard

Born on 23 January 1832, the elder son of a magistrate and a mother with diplomatic family connections. There was no parental objection to his wish to be a painter, which was quickened by his travels and experiences as a naval cadet. He entered Couture's studio, studied in the Louvre, travelled around Europe, and in 1859 offered his *Absinth Drinker* for the Salon. It was rejected. After such controversial exhibits as *Le Déjeuner sur l'Herbe* and *Olympia*, he became the hero of the younger set. Though he never exhibited with the Impressionists, he remained their champion and inspiration. He died on 30 April 1883.

Monet, Claude Oscar

Born on 14 November 1840, the son of a grocer who moved his business from Paris to Le Havre, where Monet spent his boyhood. He met Boudin who encouraged him to paint, and after military service he entered Gleyre's studio – his introduction to Renoir, Sisley and Bazille. After 1870 and an interlude in London, he went to live at Argenteuil, and there, with Renoir, brought Impressionism to a peak of brilliance and achievement. As he grew older his manner broadened into near-abstraction, ending in the spectacular water-lily paintings executed at Giverny. He died there on 5 December 1926.

Morisot. *Eugène Manet and his Daughter*, 1881. Private Collection.

Morisot, Berthe

Born on 14 January 1841, a daughter of the Prefect of Bourges. The family moved to Paris, where all the sisters took drawing lessons. Berthe, the most talented, was given painting instruction by Corot. A meeting with Manet was her introduction to the world of the Impressionists, as well as a decisive influence on her own development as a painter. She exhibited at the first Impressionist show in 1874, and in the same year married Manet's younger brother, Eugène. She was a loyal contributor to all the subsequent Impressionist exhibitions except in 1879, when she gave birth to a daughter, Julie, who in due course married the painter Georges Rouault. She died on 2 March 1895.

Pissarro, Camille

Born on 10 July 1830 in the Virgin Islands. Pissarro was sent to France as a child of twelve to complete his education. Back in the colony, his appetite for painting increased, and his parents agreed that he could return to Paris. After attending the École des Beaux-Arts and the Académie Suisse he began painting in the open air, and rapidly became a close friend of Monet and his circle. His struggles to bring his art to the high standards which he encouraged in others brought him near to despair. After a flirtation with Pointillism he reverted to the Impressionist style of the 1870s, remaining the truest of the group to the ideas which, as younger men, had bound them together. He died on 12 November 1903.

Pissarro, Lucien

Born in Paris in 1863, the eldest son of Camille Pissarro. Lucien moved to London in 1890 where he was active in the New English Art Club and in the Camden Town Group. He also made a reputation with his book printing and designs. His father's letters to him are a fruitful source of Impressionist history and ideas. He died in Heywood, Somerset, in 1944.

Redon, Odilon

Born in Bordeaux in 1840. Redon learned etching and engraving and studied at the École des Beaux-Arts in the 1860s. He became friends with Fantin-Latour, who introduced him to the Impressionist circle. His sympathies were not all with them and their ideas, however, since he inclined to the 'inner eye' concept rather than to naturalism. His ideas encouraged the growth of Symbolism in the 1890s and influenced Gauguin at a formative stage. The main impact of his highly individual manner was on Post-Impressionism. Redon died in 1916.

Renoir, Pierre Auguste

Born in Limoges on 25 February 1841. His father, a tailor, moved the family to Paris, where Renoir at first worked at a porcelain factory, decorating the wares. He spent his wages on artists' equipment, and on lessons at Gleyre's studio where he met Monet, Sisley and Bazille. With Monet he shared the golden decade of the 1870s, and regularly exhibited with the Group. Acceptance came at last, not through the Impressionists' exhibitions but at the Salon, where his portrait of Madame Charpentier and her children was shown in 1879. Renoir went his own way in the 1880s, looking for more durable forms than Impressionism offered. He died at Cagnes, his home in southern France, on 3 December 1919.

Russell, John Peter

An Australian, born in 1858, who came to London and enrolled at the Slade in 1881. He moved to Paris in 1884, was befriended by Van Gogh, and joined the circle of Rodin, Bernard and Anquetin. The main influence on his work was Monet, whom he visited in Belle-Isle, Britanny, where he made his home until 1908. He then returned to Sydney and obscurity, and died in 1930, the 'unknown Impressionist'.

Sargent, John Singer

Born in Florence on 12 January 1856, of American parents, his father being a doctor from Boston. He studied in Florence and in Paris, where in 1876 he started his career as a painter in Monet's circle. His full-length portrait of Madame Pierre Gautreau, a notable Parisienne whose affairs were the talk of society, caused a scandal when it was shown at the Salon in 1884, and virtually drove Sargent out of Paris. He settled in Chelsea, to become a brilliantly successful portrait painter of the Edwardian era and an important link between British painters and the School of Paris. He died on 18 April 1925.

Seurat, Georges

Born on 2 December 1859. Seurat studied at the École des Beaux-Arts. His first major work, *Une Baignarde*, was rejected by the Salon but exhibited at the Salon des Indépendants in 1884. The *Grande Jatte* followed at the 1886 Impressionist exhibition, Pissarro having persuaded the committee to allow the tiny group of Pointillists – himself included – to be represented. Seurat's imaginative, if restricting, advance on Impressionist principles was not well received. Seurat, however, remained true to it until his early death on 29 March 1891.

Signac, Paul

Born on 11 November 1863. Largely self-educated, he founded the Société des Artistes Indépendants with Seurat in 1884 and exhibited there until 1893. It was Signac who initiated Seurat into the techniques of Pointillism, otherwise known as Divisionism. The techniques were carried further after Seurat's death, when Signac became the leader of the Neo-Impressionists. He died on 15 August 1935.

Sisley, Alfred

Born in Paris of English parents on 30 October 1839. Sisley was essentially a French painter and belongs among the most unwavering of the Impressionists. As an early comrade of Renoir, Monet and Pissarro, he shared the struggles of the 1860s and 1870s and took part in five of the Impressionist exhibitions. He made three journeys to England, but his painting country was the landscape on the outskirts of Paris, notably Louveciennes. Monet organized a sale of his work after his death on 29 January 1899, which established his honoured position in the Impressionist circle.

Toulouse-Lautrec, Henri Marie Raymond de

Born at Albi, 24 November 1864, into an aristocratic family. Lautrec took up painting after the crippling attacks which prevented him leading an active outdoor life. He encountered the Impressionists in the 1880s, when he embarked on his famous series of studies of the denizens of Paris music-halls and brothels. He was struck by the work of Manet and Degas, in particular, and also became friendly with Van Gogh, whose move to Provence he was instrumental in bringing about. He exhibited with the Impressionists in 1889 at the Salon des Indépendents. He died on 9 September 1901.

Valadon, Suzanne

Born in 1867. An artist's model turned graphic artist and painter, she sat for Puvis de Chavannes, had a love affair with Renoir, and associated herself with Toulouse-Lautrec, through whom she attracted the attention of Degas. He admired her graphic work and remained helpful to her for the rest of his life. A later influence on her was Gauguin, some of whose energetic manner is found in her own paintings. She died in Paris in 1938.

Below:
Toulouse-Lautrec. *At the Moulin Rouge*, 1892. Narodni Galeri, Prague.

Bottom:
Bazille. *The Artist's Family on a Terrace near Montpelier*, 1867.
The artist makes a self-effacing appearance at the extreme left of this picture, which was exhibited at the Salon of 1868. Musée du Louvre, Paris.

Van Gogh, Vincent

Born on 30 March 1853 at Groot Zundert, Holland, the son of a clergyman. He turned to art in 1880, supported by his brother Theo who championed the Impressionists. Van Gogh first saw Impressionist pictures in Paris in 1886. His palette lightened, and in February 1888 he left the city for the sunnier environment of Arles. The rest of his life was the tragedy and triumph of the final two years. He shot himself at Auvers on 27 July 1890, and died two days later.

Vollard, Ambroise

A picture dealer, born in 1867, whose first coup was seeking out the all-but-unknown Cézanne in 1895 and mounting an exhibition of his work in Paris. He subsequently made a deal with the self-exiled Gauguin, then in Tahiti, to make him a regular allowance in return for his output of paintings. In 1901 he held the first exhibition of the young Picasso, who made him the subject of one of the earliest Cubist paintings. His portrait had already been painted by both Cézanne and Renoir. He died in 1938.

Whistler, James Abbot McNeill

Born at Lowell, Massachusetts and taken to St. Petersburg as a child, where his father was a consultant engineer for the St. Petersburg to Moscow railway. He was entered for West Point Academy but failed the course, and in 1855 went to Paris to study painting. He exhibited at the Salon des Refusés in 1863, along with Manet, Pissarro, Jongkind, Fantin-Latour, Guillaumin and Cézanne. Though he was never an Impressionist, his atmospheric Nocturnes share the Impressionist mood. He died in London on 17 July 1903.

Zola, Émile

Born on 2 April 1840, his critical writings and journalism did much to encourage the Impressionists in their early days. He visited the Salon des Refusés in company with his old schoolfriend, Cézanne, through whom he met Pissarro, Guillemet and others. Zola's novel *La Confession de Claude* is dedicated to Cézanne, who helped him towards a view of the artist existing by virtue of himself rather than of the subjects he chooses to paint. His views were reinforced by an acquaintance with Manet, whom he marked out for a place in the Louvre. He appears in various Impressionist paintings, including ones by Bazille and Cézanne. His portrait by Manet hangs in the Louvre. He died on 29 September 1902.

Van Gogh. *A View of Arles*, 1889. Bayerische Staatsgemäldesammlungen, Munich.

Whistler. *Miss Cecily Alexander: Harmony in Grey and Green,* 1872–4. Tate Gallery, London.

Acknowledgments

Photographs

Ashmolean Museum, Oxford 42 left
Bayerische Staatsgemäldesammlungen, Munich 78
Bildarchiv Preussischer Kulturbesitz 4–5
Courtauld Institute Galleries, London 34, 39 right, 58 top, 68
Photographie Giraudon, Paris 6, 7, 8 left, 24 right, 31, 32, 37,
39 left, 40 left, 40 right, 42 right, 44 top, 44 bottom, 45, 53,
54 top, 55 top, 55 bottom, 59 top, 70, 73 right, 74 left, 75
Hamlyn Group: John Webb 51 left, 51 right, 79
Hamlyn Group Picture Library 9 top right, 10, 11, 12, 13 top, 14, 15,
16 top, 16 bottom, 17, 18 top, 18 bottom, 19, 20, 21, 22 top,
22 bottom, 23, 25, 26, 27 bottom, 28, 29, 30 top, 30 bottom, 35, 41,
47, 52 top, 52 bottom, 56, 57 bottom left, 57 bottom right, 58 bottom,
59 bottom, 60, 61 top, 63, 64 right, 71 top, 72
Kunsthalle, Hamburg 56–57
Musée Rodin, Paris 67 left
Musées Nationaux, Paris endpapers, 2–3, 24 left, 27 top, 38,
46 bottom, 61 bottom, 65, 66, 67 right, 69 left, 77 bottom
Narodni Galeri, Prague 77 top
National Gallery, London 8–9, 9 bottom, 33 top, 33 bottom, 36, 48,
49, 69 right, 71 bottom, 73 left
National Museum of Wales, Cardiff 62
National Museum of Western Art, Tokyo 43
Ny Carlsberg Glyptotek, Copenhagen 13 bottom, 64 left
Städtische Kunsthalle, Mannheim 46 top
J. Ziolo, Paris 74 right.